PRAISE FOR
PASSAGE OF THE STORK

"Madeleine's vivid prose and extraordinary narrative technique held me spell-bound. Making uncomfortable choices and rejecting instant gratification, she set out on the quest for harmony with nature, therefore with all of life. Her journey towards this goal is inspirational."
Sabine Eiche
Writer and columnist

"Madeleine's book dances through time, describing her life journey and taking us to the mystical and meaningful undercurrent. Only we can make sense of what the rhythms of life have in store for us. An inspiring life story told by a wise woman!"
Pauline van Hezik
Certified 5Rhythms® teacher

"Madeleine shares her rites of passage with openness, deep honesty and intimacy. Her words will evoke tears, laughter, bitterness, rage, forgiveness and healing. Her story is the 'herstory' of all women who seek to live an authentic life. A must read for those who seek their soul's true design."
Robin Youngblood
Author, *Path of the White Wolf*
Traveling Ambassador, Grandmothers Circle the Earth
Wisdom Keeper, Seven Generations World Wisdom Council

"This is an account of a soul and her journey. The soul is traveling from place to place, from one feeling to another, from one life phase to the next. Passage of the Stork *is about how fate works, how life and soul lessons are learned, how a woman walks her path and how the Path walks her. Read, learn, feel. Thank you soul, for writing this book!"*
Linda Wormhoudt
Author and shamanic teacher, www.soulritual.nl

"Every now and then one comes across a narrative so honest in its depth it touches the soul of the reader. This work by Madeleine Lenagh is one such book. Using mythology and metaphor, she traces her journey of self and spiritual realization from the shy young girl to the wise elder. It is a treat to read and savor."
Melissa Usrey, M.A., MFT
Marriage and Family Therapist (retired)

PASSAGE OF THE STORK:

Delivering the Soul

One woman's journey to

self-realization

and acceptance

MADELEINE LENAGH

First Edition 2015

First Published in the United Kingdom by Springtime Books

© Copyright Springtime Books

All rights reserved. No part of this publication may be reproduced, stored in or introduced into a retrieval system, or transmitted, in any form, or by any means (electronic, mechanical, photocopying recording or otherwise) without the prior written permission of the publisher.

This book is sold subject to the condition that it shall not, by way of trade or otherwise, be lent, resold, hired out, or otherwise circulated without the publisher's prior consent in any form of binding or cover other than that in which it is published and without a similar condition including this condition being imposed on the subsequent purchaser.

The excerpt from the song *On the Other Side of Here* was used with permission from Chloe Goodchild, singer, voice teacher, and founder of The Naked Voice. Website: www.thenakedvoice.com

Design by Leigh Cann: lcann563@gmail.com

ISBN 978-0-9932377-0-6

For my grandchildren, Sara and Stan. May their lives be filled with the beauty of the world. And may they have the courage to walk their own paths in life.

ACKNOWLEDGEMENTS

I'm deeply grateful to my friends and family, who not only read and commented my unfinished drafts, but also gave me the support and encouragement I needed to get through the entire process. I'm also very grateful to Jo Parfitt and her staff at Springtime Books for their guidance along every step of the way.

My view of the world, and especially of the development of the psyche, has been influenced by many teachers along the way. Some of these provided direct inspiration for this book. I would like to name a few and recommend them to those who would like to pursue some of the themes in this book further.

The 19th century psychoanalyst and author, Carl Jung, was a major influence on modern psychology. I especially draw upon his work on archetypes, dreams, the process of individuation, and the concept of the wounded healer. In his footsteps, Joseph Campbell has explored the meaning of mythology to our modern lives.

The late Gabrielle Roth developed the practice of 5Rhythms dance, a powerful movement meditation. She has published several excellent books on the subject. However, 5Rhythms is best experienced on the dance floor. Trained teachers can be found all over the globe.

I once attended a workshop offered by NLP teacher Robert Dilts and his wife, Deborah Bacon Dilts, a 5Rhythms teacher. *The Hero's Journey*, as the workshop was titled, combined these two elements: the power of mythology and archetypes and the power of the dance. The journey I describe in this book is also a hero's journey, as are the lives of so many people. Hearing the call, leaving home, dealing with your demons, finding your helpers, reaching your goal, and returning home with your gifts.

A specific branch of psychology concerns itself with the influence of family systems, including earlier generations, on the development of the individual. My own work and insights into this field have been influenced by the Dutch shamanic teacher Daan van Kampenhout, who developed Systemic Ritual® as a shamanic approach to family constellation work.

Sensitivity was ignored by psychologists until the publication of Elaine Aron's decisive work in the 1990s. It was she who called attention to the fact that 15-20% of all people are highly sensitive and therefore easily overwhelmed. This lies at the root of many adjustment problems and traumas. But it also opens the sensitive person to subtle signals that others miss.

The Native American teacher, Robin Tekwelus Youngblood, and the above-mentioned Daan van Kampenhout, both led me on my first steps as a shamanic practitioner. But it was Linda Wormhoudt and her extensive research into the shamanic practices of Northwestern Europe, who brought me in touch with the rituals of my own ancestors from Scandinavia and the British Isles. She has written several beautiful books on the subject but they are, unfortunately, only available in Dutch. However, those wanting to know more about Ygdrassil and the three Norns would be advised to go back to the original source of our knowledge: The Edda.

ACKNOWLEDGEMENTS

Based on ancient Tibetan Buddhist practices, Tsultrim Allione developed an approach to dealing with self-destructive patterns. In her book, *Feeding Your Demons*, she describes this very accessible method.

Bill Plotkin has taken psychology and the power of non-ordinary consciousness one step further: using myth, shamanic practices, and communicating with nature, to deepen the process of personal development. The wilderness Quest I describe was done under the tutelage of Plotkin's Animas Valley Institute. I highly recommend his books and his work.

Last but certainly not least, David Whyte's evocative poetry and essays have been a major influence on my work: helping me to find my voice and to ask myself the questions that needed to be asked in order to get to the heart of the story.

To all these teachers and authors I owe a deep debt of gratitude. I have drawn heavily on their work, both in this book and in my own counseling practice.

TABLE OF CONTENTS

FOREWORD: Robin Youngblood, author of
Path of the White Wolf xiii

PREFACE xv

CHAPTER 1: PROLOGUE 1

CHAPTER 2: THE CHILD 5

CHAPTER 3: THE WOMAN 27

CHAPTER 4: THE CRONE 65

CHAPTER 5: EPILOGUE 69

BIBLIOGRAPHY AND RESOURCES 95

ABOUT THE AUTHOR 99

FOREWORD

Madeleine Lenagh is a Seeker, always searching for inner truth and understanding. She is a true Sister, gifted with loyalty, courage, honesty, wisdom, and compassion born of deep experience. In this book she shares her experience and the understanding she has gained with a desire to allow others to find their truth through her expression.

Besides being a talented storyteller, Madeleine is an amazing weaver and artist. Her artistry shows as she meshes her internal experience with the myths of the muses, her connection with the ancient witch who is both healer and destroyer. Like Spiderwoman, she weaves the web between the seen and unseen, leading us along the pathways of the conscious and unconscious – the lives we live in physical reality, and the lessons we learn through the dreamtime of our soul's journey.

I've had the honor of mentoring Madeleine as she explored certain parts of her interior landscape, and been deeply impressed by her willingness and ability to dive deeply into her inner world, while balancing a rich and active material life. Madeleine is a dancer par excellence, and her dance is evident in every area of her life. Because we identify with each other's stories, Madeleine and I have become good friends, and I know our friendship will last a lifetime or longer. As you read her tale, I think you will see yourself too, and know this Sister is a friend, whether you ever meet her in the flesh or not.

There's an old Zimbabwe adage: *If you can walk, you can dance; and if you can talk, you can sing.* I would add, where Madeleine is concerned, *If you can write, you can give the world a gift; if you have heart, you can share your story.*

Robin Youngblood
Author, *Path of the White Wolf*
Traveling Ambassador, Grandmothers Circle the Earth
Wisdom Keeper, Seven Generations World Wisdom Council

PREFACE

'My story isn't sweet and harmonious, like invented stories. It tastes of folly and bewilderment, of madness and dream, like the life of all people who no longer want to lie to themselves.'
Hermann Hesse [1]

This is a book about my own life's journey. But it could be a tale of anyone's journey: yours, your mother's or a friend's. It is a story about making choices, overcoming difficulties, and finding hope.

I was faced with the challenge of not only telling the story but, at the same time, sharing the insights I have about it now. And so I dipped into the depths of our collective unconscious: mythology, dreams and visions, and the archetypes they hold.

Musing on the need for an unbiased commentary on what was happening, an all-knowing aspect of myself, I was reminded of the chorus in classical Greek tragedies. That's when the Norns came in, mythological personages who have appeared in different guises through the ages.

We can find universal truths in the subconscious realms of myth and metaphor that help each of us see our own lives clearly. You may find yourself projecting your story onto mine and wondering if I'm describing the same thing. That is absolutely fine, it means

---

1. *Demian: The Story of Emil Sinclair's Youth* by Hermann Hesse, first published in 1919 under the pseudonym Emil Sinclair

you are engaged in the narrative and recognizing your own truth. Which is what I hope you will do: think about the path you are taking in life. Maybe you will find hope in my description of the choices I made… even those choices that seemed to be all wrong, at first.

If you find yourself looking for explanations, let the need go. Let the flow of the narrative take you deeper into the universal truths that rule all our lives. This book isn't about explanations, it's about moving on, spiraling towards who we really are.

Needless to say, I have changed the names of all the (human) protagonists in the book, in order to provide a modicum of privacy.

PASSAGE OF THE STORK:
Delivering the soul

1

PROLOGUE

MERMAID

Three mermaids play in the huge rolling waves, splashing and diving in the curling spray. Yellow light from the full Hunter's Moon breaks into tiny pieces on the restless water. The black shadow of a freighter, slowly churning its way westward, forms a speck on the reflection.

As the freighter nears the mermaids, they gaze up at the silhouettes of a man and a woman at the railing, drawing closer to each other, drinking in each other's eyes – hers are clear green, his a brilliant blue. Their hands, arms, and bodies gradually grow more and more entangled. They are oblivious to everything else.

A piece of sea foam breaks loose and drifts upwards, hovering and fluttering like a white moth, circling the couple, waiting. At the exact moment of their passionate union, it melts into the woman's body and vanishes. The mermaids sing a song of birth and love, sorrow and loss, and all the lessons a soul must learn in the space of a lifetime. A child is conceived and her life's journey commences. The mermaids slowly drift further south, away from the boat and the humans with their limited lives.

There is no sentient awareness, only a small, dark place where she swims. She's surrounded by heartbeat, pulsing the waters she swims in, echoing in her body. And the heartbeat carries another awareness, the awareness of shame. Shame and loneliness. And, even though she cannot yet give it a name, she is aware that she must carry this. It's connected to her life, her existence. She will carry it… out of love.

DROWNING

A round-faced two-year-old is playing at the water's edge on Folly Beach. The sign on the road leading to the beach reads 'The Edge of America'. The child's reddish-brown curls tumble around her head. She loves the way the Atlantic waves crash around her and cover her with salt spray. The way the undertow pulls the sand out from under her toes, tickling her feet and making leaf-like patterns.

Her mother stretches out on a blanket, up on the dry sand, chatting happily with wives of other naval officers and throwing occasional flirtatious glances at the lifeguard, high in his white, wooden tower. She is well aware of the effect her beauty has on men.

No one sees the large wave catch the child and knock her down. No one sees the treacherous undertow pull her body into the deep water.

She doesn't fight the wave, she doesn't scream. She surrenders to the urgent sea, letting her body go limp, tumbling around and around, lungs filling with ocean. She reaches out, reaching for the bright light shining through the green water, reaching for the mermaids and the song they sing to her, welcoming her back.

And then, suddenly, hands are pulling at her, she's on the hot sand, her throat filled with a vile, acrid taste, voices shouting.

Several months later, she's on an ocean liner with her mother and stepfather, heading for France. On the deck, she hangs over the railings, watching the ship endlessly roll on the Atlantic

CHAPTER 1 – PROLOGUE

waves, feeling the spray blowing through her curls, waving to the mermaids who wave back to her. She will always love the sea but she will retain a fear of drowning.

The spreading ash tree reaches down with three large roots into the Underworld. It is called Ygdrassil, the Tree of Life. The tips of its branches disappear into the heavens. A stern eagle perches in its lower branches, white tail and yellow curved beak just barely visible.

At the foot of the tree, three women sit next to bottomless Urd's well. There are many names for these ancient women, but in the Nordic tradition they are known as the Norns, the spinners and weavers of the wyrd, or fate, of humans.

The first woman is old and bent, her long white hair flows over her shoulders and she holds a wooden spindle in her hands. She plucks starlight and sea foam, grasses and flowers, hairs from the chins of witches and feathers from the wings of birds. All these she uses to spin her thread. Urd is her name, like the name of the well. She presides over That Which Had to Be.

The second woman is buxom and radiates health and vitality. Her sky-blue robes complement her dark eyes and auburn hair. She is called Verdandi and she presides over That Which Is Coming to Be. She takes the woven thread and weaves it into complex patterns on her large wooden loom.

The third woman's face is hidden behind a long white veil. She wears a sharp knife at her leather belt, blade and hilt beaten out of the same piece of iron. She is Skuld. Her domain is That Which

Will Have to Be. She occasionally gets up and goes to the tree to carve runes into its thick bark.

"Sisters, I feel sorry for this little creature of the sea." *Verdandi studies the web she's weaving intently.* "She carries her mother's shame. She's in for a great deal of pain."

"That will make her strong. Pain is part of her life's journey. She will need to face it if she is going to follow her wyrd," *Skuld mutters and carves* ᚦ *Thurisaz, the rune of suffering, sharply into the wood.*

Urd only smiles, twirling her spindle endlessly on her lap, spinning her thread.

2
THE CHILD

ᚠ

FEAR

Big hairy arms and a body smelling of freshly ironed cloth pick me up and plant me in the wooden high chair. I sense fumbling at the straps that keep me from climbing down to freedom. A bowl of hot, sweet cereal lands in front of me.

No! No cereal! Book! I lift up the cloth book dangling in my sweaty fist, the book with the pretty elephant, to show him. The book lands in the cereal. Suddenly my hand is grabbed and the book is wrenched out of it. "No! Book! Book!"

The unfamiliar, deep voice scares me. "You can't have the book until you've eaten your oatmeal! Now hurry up and eat, I have to leave in ten minutes!"

A spoonful of hot sticky stuff is forced against my lips. I kick and turn my head away.

"No!" The cereal lands in my curly hair.

The man, whom I would later learn to call Daddy, curses and grabs my arm. No one ever says "no" to him. I start screaming.

"Dammit! Eat your oatmeal!" he roars. He grabs the bowl of cereal. Suddenly it's soaring towards me. I wince and try to pull away. The bowl strikes my forehead and the hot oatmeal drips down my face.

The bedroom door bangs open and my mother runs out, still in her nightgown, rubbing sleep out of her eyes. "Frank! What the hell are you doing! Get away from my daughter!"

I hold my arms out to her. Mummy's here. It will be alright now. She holds a cloth under the kitchen faucet and starts cleaning the cereal off my sobbing face.

The irate man turns and walks out the front door, slamming the screen.

There's a photograph of me as a three-year-old, standing in the middle of a courtyard of the Alhambra. In the pale January sun, I'm dressed in a little Loden coat with a double row of toggle-buttons. I'm oblivious to the graceful Moorish arches and beautiful mosaics. I'm screaming with terror, the courtyard is filled with flies and they keep landing on me. Daddy shouts at me to stop being so silly. It just makes me scream harder.

We live in Europe for three years, moving from Paris, France, to Bad Homburg, Germany, and then on to Hampstead Heath, London. Daddy has been sent to work at the NATO as a Naval attaché. When I'm five years old, we board the *Île de France* once more to return to the States and settle down in Westport, Connecticut. Mummy is pregnant with the first of my siblings: Kate. She will soon be followed by little Frankie and, some years later, by Annie. Daddy exchanges his Navy career for a job on Wall Street and starts commuting to New York every day.

He comes in the kitchen door, calling out to whomever will listen, bigger than life and much more threatening. Before I can get away, he scoops me up and plants me on top of the refrigerator.

"What are you doing up there?" he shouts with laughter at his own joke. I whimper and wave my arms, begging to be let down.

"Mummy!" I wail.

"Mummies are in the tombs of Egypt!" he roars again.

CHAPTER 2 - THE CHILD

"Stop teasing the child," my mother snaps.

He turns and stalks into the living room.

My mother puts up her arms, lets me slide into them and down on to the floor. "Now stop crying," she admonishes. She wipes my tears gently and turns back to her stove.

In the stone steps leading up to the front door of our house, there's a little, fairy-sized hollow in the upright section of the step. I lie on my stomach, hearing gossamer wings rush by. Carefully, I lay out long pieces of grass, just the right size to harness fairy horses to a chariot.

Inside, I hear the heavy steps of my stepfather approaching. Panic overtakes me and I jump up and run away, across the driveway, up the hill, brushing past the grasses and tall sumac bushes with their red leaves and spikes of little crimson berries, up along a path cut by the gardener last spring. Here I'm safe, no one ever comes looking for me up here. I fall onto the grass, resting my back against a smooth beech trunk. Tall cedar trees sway gently, rocking the red-wing blackbirds with their bright splash of color.

The birds sing to me, "Come fly with us, there's nothing to be afraid of!"

The mermaid pulls herself up on to the rock and looks up at the stars. As her tail swishes gently in the water, bright phosphorescence swirls and coils in its wake. She starts to sing, softly at first but then her voice starts to ring out, like a clear bell. She sings of loneliness, of longing for love.

At Urd's Well, Skuld hears the sweet tones of the mermaid's song. She smiles a secret smile behind her white veil and pulls her knife from its leather sheath. She carves the rune

ᚾ Naudhiz: *need, onto the tree. She hesitates and then carves*
ᛉ Algiz, *meaning protection.*

SAFE HAVEN

My haven away from the turmoil at home is Grandmother's house. I call her Grandmother, just as Mummy always calls her Mother. It fits her tiny, erect figure, platinum hair swept up in a bun, the fashionable frizz on her forehead, and her aristocratic silver cigarette holder.

A fiercely independent woman, she went through tuberculosis and the death of her father at a young age, and subsequently fell in love with an Army lieutenant without telling her mother. When he was sent to France to fight in WWI, she signed up as a nurse for the Red Cross and traveled to France to find him. She found her lieutenant and they married in France. They returned to the States, mollified her indignant mother, and built a beautiful large house in Chappaqua, Westchester County, New York. Their happiness was short-lived; he died in a hunting accident in 1932, leaving her with five children, including my eight-year-old mother. The term 'hunting accident' is hers. He was alone with his rifle, it went off, and killed him. Grandmother never remarried.

I often spend the weekend with her and her collection of long-haired black cats. Witchwood, as the house in the Connecticut woods is named, is my second home. I spend hours on the large yellow damask upholstered couch, reading the old books in the cedar built-in bookcases that line any wall not filled with a floor-length window. My favorite book is a 1932 edition of *Folk Tales and Fairy Lore in Gaelic and English*, a compilation of Scottish legends. It is here that I have my first conscious out-of-body experience, feeling suspended up near the ceiling and

CHAPTER 2 - THE CHILD

watching my body lie, hot and feverish, on the couch. Somehow this feels right, my body is just an uncomfortable encumbrance.

Now I'm sitting at a little desk in the art studio. The desk was built for me by my uncle and is just my size. Grandmother has given me a pile of pale green ceramic tiles. After a few false starts, I'm painstakingly painting a Siamese cat with oil colors on a tile. Mummy likes Siamese cats, we have two at home. Every once in a while, I glance at the black long-haired beauties twining around my legs and sleeping at my feet, to get the proportions right.

"Excellent, Maddy!" Grandmother rests her hand on my shoulder. "Now let it dry and you can give it to your mother when you go home."

At home, I proudly hand Mummy her present, chattering away to her about my weekend with Grandmother. She glances at the painted tile and nods absentmindedly, as she carefully guides the material for a new dress through the sewing machine.

"Very nice dear. And have you practiced your violin?"

I work hard at the etudes my violin teacher has given me. Downstairs I hear Mummy's voice calling up, "That sounds pretty flat to me, try it again!" I give up and pick out a Brahms tune that I like, by ear.

"I don't think she gave you that one. You don't want to annoy her, she believes in your talent but you need to practice!"

I go back to my etudes, I'm a little afraid of my violin teacher with her sharp tongue and endless anecdotes of past concert-hall fame.

Enchantment

For Christmas, Mummy gives me two beautifully illustrated volumes of Homer's *Iliad* and *Odyssey*, abridged for young readers. I'm entranced by the stories. I weep at the death of

Hector, gasp with horror at the interventions of the sea god Poseidon, and fall in love with faithful and resourceful Penelope. My mother takes her old editions of Frazer's *Golden Bough* and Sturluson's *Prose Edda* down from the bookcase for me to read too. When I have gone through all the Greek and Nordic mythology she can find, I start in on her collection of Sir Walter Scott's novels.

At school my mother is admonished for giving me adult books to read.

"I know she's only ten years old. But she reads everything she can get her hands on. She always has her nose in a book!"

"Yes, but Maddy's grades are poor," the teacher points out. "She spends her time daydreaming and reading instead of paying attention. She's intelligent enough but she needs to apply herself. And she never plays with other children, she's always off in her own world."

Our big white-shingled house with its black shutters, set back on a lawn dotted with apple and maple trees, is a place of magic and mystery. In my bedroom closet, a mysterious ledge intrigues me. What or whom is it hiding? Is there a treasure in there?

The wooden-beamed attic does contain treasures: brass-studded black trunks filled with my mother's old dresses, the perfect attire for a mermaid princess. I can play up there for hours.

A mysterious fist-sized hole in the attic floor, covered with a wooden lid, gives way to a long pipe that goes all the way down through the house. If I throw something in, it lands on the cellar floor. I send secret messages down and retrieve them quickly before anyone reads them.

My mother takes us off on long jaunts: wildflower-picking, bird-watching, rock-hunting in the Connecticut hills where we

CHAPTER 2 - THE CHILD

find beautiful dark-green tourmaline crystals. And, though I prefer being on my own, these adventures strengthen my love for all the inhabitants of the natural world.

One warm spring day, I pack a lunch and a little red bucket and go exploring the brook on the other side of the road. I want to find its source. I follow it upstream as far as I can go, sometimes clambering on the banks and sometimes splashing through the water. Eventually, the brook disappears in an underground culvert. In a quiet pool, I find frogs' eggs. I carefully tip them into the bucket and bring them home, filling the bathtub in my own bathroom with water and sliding the eggs in. To my delight, a few days later I have tadpoles in the bathtub. Mummy does not share my delight.

"Maddy, the tadpoles do not belong in the bathtub! No wonder you kept using ours. Take them outside and put them into the pond!"

"Yes, Mummy." I trudge upstairs and remove the tadpoles to the large marshy pond at the edge of our property.

LIFE AND DEATH

It's a luscious, warm spring day and I'm lying on my belly in the grass, watching birds fly on and off at the feeder next to the dining-room window. Our Siamese cat comes around the corner of the garage, emitting a strangled meow as if he is carrying something in his mouth. I look up and gasp, a baby robin is struggling between his jaws. At my shout, he drops the bird and slinks away. I run over and cup my hands gently under the bird, lifting it up from the grass.

"Mummy, Koko caught a baby robin and she's still alive!" My mother steps out of the kitchen door, drying her hands on her apron, and inspects the fluffy little, orange-breasted bird, panting in my hands. "She seems to be okay. Why don't you try giving her water with a little dropper?"

I drip water carefully into her beak and she eagerly opens it wide for more. I put her in a shoebox with some dried grasses to lie on.

"May I keep her in my room? Otherwise the cat will get her again," I plead.

"That's fine with me, if you take responsibility for feeding her. And when she's better, you will have to let her go. She's meant to be free."

The idea of picking up worms horrifies me, so I pay my enterprising little brother a dime for every earthworm he digs out of the huge mulch pile behind the garage. Then I transport the worm, gingerly, with tweezers, to the open beak of the baby bird, who *peep-peeps* demandingly every time I come into the bedroom.

She's quite unafraid of me and, after a few days, starts hopping onto my open hand. I take her up onto the bed and let her flutter off my hand. Each day I can hold her higher and her wings grow stronger.

"Mummy, I think she can fly tomorrow. Shall I take her out then and set her free?"

The next morning I open my eyes and turn to look at my little friend in her shoebox. She is lying with her tiny curled feet up in the air, quite stiff. I go running down the stairs, my feet thudding on the green carpet, screaming and sobbing.

"I'm so sorry, my dear. Probably she had an injury we couldn't see that opened up again when she started flying. Now take her out and bury her somewhere." My mother's voice is gentle and I hear sadness behind her words.

I take the shoebox with my dead baby up to my sanctuary on the hill and sit with her until my tears no longer flow. Then I dig a hole and bury her carefully, asking the redwing-blackbirds and cedar trees to take care of her.

The sisters of the wyrd are seated under Ygdrassil's wide branches. Verdandi's shuttle flies back and forth on her loom. She strokes the texture of the work she has just finished and then turns and calls to the others.

"Sisters, this child is starting to grow into a woman. It's time she starts learning to bear her pain."

Skuld silently extracts her knife from her belt and carves the rune ᛚ Laguz: chaos, potential, onto the wood of the tree of life.

Awkward adolescence

Gym class, the most dreaded time of the school day. We're lined up at the softball field and I'm keeping as far back as possible while the team captains start taking turns choosing kids. I'll get picked last. I'm of no use to the team, I can't run fast, I can't throw a ball, and when the ball comes towards me I wince and look away.

The teams start filling up. Just me and two others left. I wish I were invisible. Then just me. The last team captain sighs, "Okay, her." I sidle over to the team and hope that the hour will go quickly.

The sun rises slowly through the birch and pines on the shores of Mount Desert Island. Dawn has already started as a cobalt blue wash, turning the calm sea and craggy Maine hills into a magical place. Now rays of sun are hitting the houses and the rocks, turning everything golden.

Lobster boats chug slowly and noisily, pulling up their traps, followed by hordes of mewling gulls who fight over every floating object that looks edible. On the docks, empty lobster traps dry in the sun, barnacles clinging to their algae-stained, slatted sides. The air is filled with the silt stench of mudflats and the tangy scent of pine forests.

Up above a rocky beach, my family's heavy cotton tent is perched at the edge of the woods. I trudge along the shoreline, studying the stones and slipping the prettier ones into my pocket. A faded blue and green dinghy is pulled up above the seaweed-strewn tideline. Later that day, Daddy lugs out the outboard motor and attaches it to the stern.

"Come on, get in the boat! We're going fishing!"

I drag my feet and try to ignore him.

"You too, Maddy!"

Mummy stays back at the tent, caring for Annie, the new baby.

'Fishing', he calls it. He throws his lures out, the two younger children squabble and splash, scaring all the fish away. I trail my fingers in the water and dream of caverns beneath the sea, filled with mermaids, mermen, and jewel-colored fish. After an hour or so, he hauls in his lines.

"Now jump in for a swim," he commands. The little water-rats squeal with pleasure. Five-year-old Frankie, his chipmunk-round cheeks red with excitement, tumbles over the side. Quickly followed by Kate, her braids flying and green eyes snapping. I let myself slip, gingerly, into the icy-cold Atlantic water and dog-paddle around the dinghy. Then, treading water slowly, I stay out of sight of the others.

"Time to get back in the boat, your mother has dinner ready." His voice booms out over my head.

CHAPTER 2 - THE CHILD

The children clamber back into the boat, laughing and gasping as they tumble over the gunwales. I put my hands on the rim and try to pull myself up. The boat rocks and water splashes over my head. I choke as I accidentally swallow some and fight down rising panic.

"Come on, hippo! Get into the boat!" He glares at me, not offering to help. I'm struggling. My puny arms are helpless and my knees slip on the slimy hull. Finally, I heave a leg up and over the gunwale and pull myself over.

Slinking into the bow, coiled ropes cutting into my bare legs, I glare sullenly at him as he vainly pulls and pulls at the ignition cord of the outboard. Finally the motor turns over and we silently make our way back to the beach. As soon as the boat hits the rocky bottom, I slip over the side and start running.

"Maddy! Get back here! Help me put the boat away! Maddy!"

I ignore him and run up into the woods. I lean my head against the smooth white bark of a birch. The tree sways and murmurs to me but a voice inside me keeps saying, *Hippo! He's right. I'm stupid. I'm fat. I'm clumsy.*

The family is spending the day at Westport's pebble and shell covered Compo Beach. The younger children have taken buckets and shovels to the water's edge, building intricate castles, battlements, and moats on the strips of sand made visible at low tide. Mummy and I are lounging on green and white striped canvas beach chairs with a blue refrigerator box containing lunch between us. The homemade zucchini bread is delicious and I break off another piece.

Mummy frowns. "You know those paintings by Rubens? You don't want to grow up looking like that, do you?"

I stare down glumly at my teenage body with its rounded feminine forms. My breasts are too large. My back and shoulders slump. My mother is slim, elegant, and erect. I adore her. She's impossibly beautiful, the way movie actresses are beautiful, and she's charming and creative. I try so hard to meet up to her expectations. When I grow up, I want to be just like her. I'm sure that's impossible.

ADORATION TURNS TO ANGER

I curl up on my parents' big four-poster bed, gazing adoringly up at my mother. This is our special time, after the younger children have gone off to bed. The only time of day that I have her undivided attention. I ply her with questions and she tells me tales of her own youth: about the time she rubbed herself with poison ivy so everyone would feel sorry for her, about the death of her father and how she saw a white dove flying up the chimney at the exact moment that it happened, about her beautiful white horse she named Sugar Baby.

One evening I ask her, "Mummy, how did you meet Daddy?"

She sighs and doesn't answer for a moment. "I knew you would ask this question one day. You see, Maddy, I used to be married to someone else. I left my first husband when I was pregnant with you and came back to live with you at your grandmother's house. I met Frank when you were two years old."

The words don't register immediately. Then I gasp and my mind starts spinning. *He's not my father! Of course he isn't! I knew it!*

I sit up and face her. "Why didn't you tell me?" My voice sounds a bit shrill.

She looks away, "We thought it was better to let you grow up believing that he is your father. He's been a father to you in all ways and loves you as much as his own children." I push away the anger that is starting to fill me up, like water rising.

"Who's my real father?"

She starts mumbling, her words ambiguous. A name I don't

CHAPTER 2 - THE CHILD

recognize. A beatnik life in Greenwich Village, both living as artists. Something about a trip to China to make a documentary movie, something about a cameraman and a *ménage à trois*.

I don't understand but I don't want to confront her. "Can I meet him sometime?"

"My first husband?" She gazes at me with big eyes. "He's never asked about you, never been interested in finding out who you are."

That night I can't sleep. They lied to me! They've been lying to me for years!

I start having recurring dreams, dreams so vivid that they haunt me during the day.

> *The witch comes creeping up the stairs of the house, her dark cloak blending into the night. I'm sitting on the landing, peering down. I can't see her but I know she's there. I shrink back, up the few steps to the top. If I move quietly, I can reach my bedroom without her catching me. The witch smiles and waits patiently. Sooner or later, I will be hers.*

The dark-haired man lets the screen door of the kitchen slam behind him. He tosses his Navy duffle bag and white captain's cap into the corner where Mummy will later patiently remove the laundry and tidy things up. Even though he has left the Navy, he still belongs to the Navy Reserve and captains a destroyer escort several weekends a year. My brother, sisters and I exchange glances and quietly melt away, upstairs to our rooms.

Ten minutes later a voice booms through the house.

"Rooms ready for inspection!"

"I'm too old for this nonsense! Besides, he's not even my real father," I groan to the blue and white paisley bedspread. I glance around at the clothing scattered in the corner, the books and papers all over my bed and desk. Then I pick up my book and continue to read.

His heavy steps come up the stairs and suddenly he's in my room. He glances around and his face darkens. I lift my chin defiantly. Wordlessly, he strides the two steps to my bed and grabs my arm, fumbling at his black leather belt, his favorite weapon of punishment.

My anger growls and spits like a snarling cat.

I do NOT have to put up with this! I bring his hand to my mouth and bite down on his wrist, as hard as I can.

My stepfather freezes for a moment, staring at me. The few seconds feel like the birth of the universe. Then he drops my arm, wheels around and stalks out of the room. I hear his steps thump up to the top floor, hear his voice yelling at my brother.

My fury leaves me as abruptly as it came. Walking on trembling legs, I make my way down to the kitchen. My mother is standing at the counter, patiently kneading bread.

"Mummy, I just bit Daddy."

Mummy looks up briefly with a little smile. "Good for you!"

I walk out of the house quietly and make my dazed way up the hill to my secret sanctuary.

"That man is never going to hit me again," I vow to the patient, tall cedar trees.

The trees whisper to me that everything will be alright.

Escape

I get sent off to boarding school. "It will provide you with a much higher quality of education than the local high-school," my mother explains.

It feels like banishment.

CHAPTER 2 - THE CHILD

My grandmother whispers to me, "Don't worry, it will take you far away from all the fights at home."

I kneel and slip my hand under the mattress of my bed, searching. I hear footsteps coming down the long hallway and jerk my hand back, sitting up straight on the bed. The door to our room opens and my roommate walks in, without her usual boisterous jesting.

"Mrs. Spencer wants to see you," she says, unbuttoning her coat and tossing it onto her bed.

I look up sharply but her eyes avoid mine. She changes into the starchy cotton domestic work uniform that barely covers her knobby knees, and tucks lank, dun hair beneath the drawstring cap. I watch her fingers fumble with the double row of buttons. She leaves the room for our daily hour of domestic work and I hear the click of the door falling into the latch.

I tie on my sturdy shoes, stand up, and smooth my jeans skirt down below my knees. Even though Northfield School for Girls does not have uniforms, there are strict dress codes. I leave the room, walking slowly through the long hallway with its pale green walls and swinging glass door, down two flights of stairs. The door to the office of the dormitory mistress is to the left of the front door. The door is always open so she can see who goes in and out. The school encourages us to call them dorm mothers. Mrs. Spencer is anything but motherly.

Moving slowly, I enter the office. Pale grey-blue eyes stare at me coldly over the gold rims of her eyeglasses.

"Close the door and sit down," she snaps.

I perch myself across from her on a narrow-backed chair with a slidy seat. Then I see what's lying on the large, cherry desk in front of her: three slim, green, hard-backed books. I don't need to read the cover to know what is written on it: *Chronicles of Narnia* by C.S. Lewis. My cheeks flame. I drop my eyes to the patterns on the plush yellow Chinese carpet. Round and round they swirl, like waves on the sea.

"Fortunately, your roommate is an honest girl and didn't want you to get into any more trouble than you're already in. So she came and told us what she'd found under your bed."

My eyes lift to Mrs. Spencer's pearl necklace.

"It's bad enough that you stole them but you defaced them as well!" Her voice is icy. She flips open the top volume and pushes it across towards me. I take it and gaze at the black and white drawing, carefully and lovingly colored in with brilliant colors from my pencil set.

"We have, of course, written to your parents. You've forfeited your fall weekend home. This is a bad start to your junior year."

My eyes move past her to the tall window across the room. Crimson maple trees blaze in the New England autumn sun. I hardly see them.

"I talked to the school library. They agree that 20 hours of work in the library is a fair way to pay back the cost of the books. Besides, it will teach you to respect library books. Oh, and I have arranged for you to talk with the school counselor."

My eyes drop to the book in my hands. I stroke the pages longingly.

"I think it's probably time for your next class. You may leave the books here."

"Yes, Mrs. Spencer," I whisper and then slowly, reluctantly slide the book back onto her desk.

Finally, during my senior year, I start to love the school and my precious time away from home. My mind is on fire. We discuss Sartre and Camus in French. I take Asian Studies and read the *Upanishads*. In advanced placement English class we write poetry and short stories. I listen to Pete Seeger and Joan Baez sing

CHAPTER 2 - THE CHILD

protest songs, discard my violin, and buy a guitar. I teach myself to play and I sing Bob Dylan's *The Times, They Are A-Changin'*.

During art class, I try to emulate my mother's delicate drawings of flowers and birds. But my work is clumsy and the art teacher ignores me. I take up photography instead.

This is also the year I discover boys. Ours is an all-girls school but the brother school is a few miles away and social events are held regularly. To my surprise, in spite of my shyness, the stream of invitations is steady. Boys are the main topic of conversation during late-night giggles with my roommate.

Now, at home for the summer, I feel constrained. This morning at the breakfast table, the conversation shifts to a report of a girl being raped at the high school in a nearby town. My sister Kate and I express our horror.

My mother sniffs. "If Maddy were being raped, she'd probably lie back and enjoy it." Her caustic and casual remark slices into my heart.

I stare at her with my mouth open, but she avoids my gaze. Asking to be excused, I take my plate to the kitchen and leave the house, seeking the solace of the woods and the companionship of the birds. I fight a sense of confusion and shame. Is there something wrong with me that I cannot see and she can?

The mermaid sings to me, songs of yearning for love and belonging, songs of loneliness. I have forgotten how to hear her but her songs dwell in my eyes and hair, drip from my fingers, fuel my restless dreams.

THE MESSENGER

I lounge with my girlfriend, Sally, at Compo Beach's pavilion, a wooden structure with peeling grey paint and picnic tables. Two bored 17-year-olds, hanging out for the summer, trying to look sophisticated. Sally's slanted green eyes open wide as we hear the sound of two large motorcycles approaching.

"Take a look at the hunks getting off those bikes," she whispers excitedly.

We straighten up as they approach. Helmetless, they brush their long hair out of their eyes and smile at us. I can't stop looking at the taller one in jeans, tanned, golden hair tumbling down to his shoulders. I'm sure they're both much older than we are.

"You guys must be from out of town," Sally calls out in her most honeyed voice, tossing her blond bob. "I would have recognized those gorgeous bikes, otherwise."

The shorter, dark-haired man smiles. "Actually, my parents live near here. But I live in California now. Troy and I are taking a road trip across country and I decided to drop in and visit my folks."

We chat and I try to look casual. Then Troy turns to me.

"You wouldn't happen to be able to recommend a good place to eat, would you? I want to let Steve have some time alone with his family this evening."

My cheeks flood. "My mother enjoys visitors, you might even be able to come and have supper with us. Shall I call her and see?"

"I would be honored!"

I go find a pay phone and return a few minutes later. "Mummy says it's fine with her."

"Then I'll give you a lift home, how would you like that?"

I can't believe my good fortune. I gingerly step onto the motorcycle and, after being encouraged to do so, wrap my arms around his waist. As we pull out, Sally waves and gives me a huge wink.

At home, Troy captivates my mother with his good manners and tales of cross-country traveling. He calls her 'Ma'am' and her cheeks color pink, laughing like a young girl. I sit out on the porch with him while we wait for her to finish preparing dinner. We sip homemade lemonade and I sit on the floor at his feet

CHAPTER 2 - THE CHILD

while he praises my beautiful, big blue eyes. As I tell him my yearning for new places, new experiences, anywhere but here, his face grows serious.

"There's a book you should read, *Siddhartha* by Hermann Hesse." He goes on to describe the life of Siddhartha, how he searches for happiness his entire life and finally finds it as a simple ferryman on the river.

I listen, entranced, a world opening up to me that is deeper and wider than anything I have experienced before.

After dinner I walk with him to his motorcycle on the driveway.

"Farewell blue eyes! Follow your dreams… and don't forget to read that book!" He kisses me on the forehead and I watch as he roars off.

FIRST LOVE

It's 1968, I have just turned 19 and I'm in my second year at Antioch College. I change the spelling of my nickname to Maddi, Maddy seems so commonplace. I wear flowers in my long, wavy hair and my favorite perfume is patchouli oil. My education consists primarily of the dreamy world of psychedelic drugs and even dreamier meanderings in nature. I march in demonstrations: against the war in Vietnam, against persecution and bigotry at home. Everywhere else in the world looks better than being in the USA.

Sam has not yet turned 18, is finishing high school, and living with his mother. He wants to go to Art College. I am awed by his abstract paintings and his dedication to art and music. He looks like George Harrison and is the handsomest and most romantic man I have ever met.

The first night we make love, I get up and stand naked at the window. I reach out, pull down the moon, and give it to him. We teach each other everything we know about sex and then find ways to learn more together. I leave college to be close to him. We move to Provincetown and find jobs at a local restaurant. We rent a room that reminds us of the movie, *Elvira Madigan*. Life is perfect.

I take him home to meet my mother. She's very polite to him. But, somehow, her every word and gesture seem to speak disapproval. I fight her unspoken judgment but rapidly lose the battle. I need her approval and am lost without it.

"Your mother called when you were out. She had a long talk with me. Maybe she's right, maybe you deserve a better person than me."

"What did she say?" I ask frantically.

"She said I'm a young lout, what do I know about love?" He turns away.

Verdandi turns to look at Urd. "Why did she let him go so easily?"

Urd chuckles and twirls her spindle even faster. "She doesn't know that herself. But he's only in her life to show her the next step of the way."

"Why did you do that!" I scream at my mother. "You had no right to tear us apart like that!"

She gazes at me pensively with narrowed green eyes. "You deserve much better than that lout. I have introduced you to several nice young men. They go to good colleges and come from good families. Why don't you date them?"

"I don't want your *nice young men*! They're boring!" I turn my back on her and start gathering my things.

My stepfather speaks up from the dining room, where he has been reading the Sunday papers all morning, "Then go back to

CHAPTER 2 - THE CHILD

college! You're throwing away your intelligence and your good education!" His voice travels after me as I trudge up the stairs to my room.

Sam and I had always planned to go to Europe together. I go alone. I travel through France, Austria, Yugoslavia, Italy, and back up through Germany. My money runs out in the Netherlands and I find a job as an au pair. I sell my airline ticket to buy winter clothing. I never get around to leaving.

In a clearing in an ancient forest, a wooden hut stands on chicken legs. The hut is surrounded by a fence made of human bones and topped by skulls. As evening falls, the eyes of the skulls begin to glow. The ground shakes, the forest groans, and the door of the hut flies open. The witch peers around the edge of the door. In the folklore of the Slavic countries she is known as Baba Yaga. Her greasy grey hair is tucked under a bright red, embroidered kerchief but strays of hair escape and fall down along her wart-covered face.

She sniffs the air with her long, crooked nose. She smiles a fierce smile and gives a sharp whistle. Around, from in back of the hut, a large wooden mortar and pestle come flying to her. She hops into the mortar and sits astride the pestle, pulling up her long grey skirts. Then she whistles again and a long broom comes flying out of the forest into her outstretched hand.

　　"Let's get to work!" she cackles. "This girl needs to start learning about power!"

At Urd's well, Skuld takes her knife from her belt and walks to the huge, scarred ash tree, where she carves the rune ᚱ *Raidho:*

Momentum. Then she produces an iron cup from within the folds of her long skirts and dips it into the well. She pours a libation out at the foot of the tree and returns to her seat.

3

THE WOMAN

Finding a home

Opening night at the new youth center in Vijfhuizen is crowded and chaotic. I'm there with a group of volunteer filmmakers to make a documentary of the festivities. The line up features hot new music groups like The Bintangs and people have come from as far away as Amsterdam to listen.

I feel overwhelmed by the noise, the crowd filled with unfamiliar faces, and the smell of too many bodies in a closed space. As I stumble on the steep steps going down into the crowd, I let the borrowed 8mm movie camera fall out of my hands and watch, with dismay, as it bounces down the stairs.

Suddenly, a booming male voice addresses me in English. I straighten up and meet the cheerful brown eyes of a friendly man with a heavy American accent, who hands the camera back to me.

"Hi! You must be the other expat! I've heard about you. I'm Brian, the Navy deserter, I'm sure you've read about me."

I immediately feel at home with him. He introduces me to his companion, Anco, a quiet blond man carrying a Leica. He's the event photographer. We smile at each other shyly. I like his gentle face and the fact that he's a photographer.

"I did a lot of photography before I left the States. But I no longer have a darkroom, unfortunately." I look away so he won't see me blushing.

"You're welcome to use mine." Anco fumbles in his pocket, tears off the flap of a packet of tobacco-rolling papers, borrows a pen, and writes down his name, address, and phone number for me.

I write my mother weekly, long letters about my life in the Netherlands. I stress my success and describe in glowing terms my introduction to the world of artists and photographers. A desire to go to art school has awakened but I don't believe that I have enough talent. Mummy writes back, proud I'm making a life for myself, encouraging me to take advantage of this wonderful opportunity.

At Christmas, I take Anco back to the States to meet the family. To my surprise, my mother greets him with enthusiasm, using her charm to pull him out of his shy reticence and talk about his work. As we sit in the cedar-paneled library, around the Christmas tree, my mother unwraps the large black-and-white photographic prints he has brought as gifts.

"Oh my goodness, these are absolutely beautiful! You have such talent!" she exclaims.

He shuffles his feet and apologizes for not having had them framed properly. She pulls out her 1953 Leica and they compare notes on photography. My stepfather grumbles at our sharing a bedroom but, for the rest, ignores us.

As the date for our return to the Netherlands approaches, I begin to worry whether I will be granted a new resident's visa. "I don't have a job and I can't claim that I'm a student."

Anco clears his throat. "We could get married," he says awkwardly.

Dilapidated brick houses border narrow, cobbled streets in this part of Haarlem's old town center. The neighborhood is on the

CHAPTER 3 - THE WOMAN

'wrong' side of the river and lacks the quaint historical charm so typical of this medieval town. Primarily populated by a mixture of cast-offs and young people looking for affordable housing in the 1970s, the neighborhood is a forgotten place.

Our house consists of a shop front downstairs, grimy from its years of use as a motorcycle repair shop, two large rooms upstairs and an attic up steep, rickety stairs. We bought it for a song, but it needs a tremendous amount of work. We live on Anco's infrequent freelance assignments. While my husband scours junkyards and building sites for material to use, I tear out the concrete in the backyard with a crowbar and start a garden. I buy wooden shoes and paint them sky blue.

My sewing machine is the old-fashioned kind that works with a foot treadle. We found it in a junkyard and brought it home so I could make my own clothes. Making my own clothes seems – to me – to be the epitome of a romantic domestic life. I guide the needle carefully through the blue cotton material. And then, for the tenth time that evening, the thread snags and breaks. Cursing, I pull the spool of thread off the top spindle and hurl it through the room. I'm wasting my time, my good education, my intelligence, and my life! Anco sniggers and I glare at him. At that moment, the clanging of the doorbell breaks the tension.

Anco runs down the long narrow staircase and comes back up with two young men, dressed in suits. They perch on our worn, second-hand chairs and introduce themselves as architects, hoping to get neighborhood residents interested in positive action for urban renewal.

They unfold large drawings. "If the city government has its way, this block of buildings will be torn down to make space for a parking garage, serving the downtown area."

I explode indignantly, "These plans are totally illogical!

They should be investing in the old neighborhoods, not tearing them down!"

The men look at me with interest. Anco excuses himself and disappears into his darkroom. I put my name down on a list of people willing to take action.

Pandora's box

In the bare, grey room of the college in The Hague, our psychology professor looks around at the expectant faces of the group.

My activities in the neighborhood have inspired me to go back to school and study community work. I will drive down with two other students from Haarlem twice a week. Today is our first day and we have been meeting with each of our professors to hear what will be expected of us. I'm surprised to discover there are very few requirements and no exams until the final year, when we will be interviewed on our thesis. The school seems to believe our work experience (in my case volunteer work) will give us enough material to learn from.

This teacher seems to have other things in mind. He starts a long discourse on Carl Jung, Fritz Perls, Carl Rogers, and other great names in psychology. He assumes we are familiar with their work and have been reading up on them.

I raise my hand hesitantly and he stops talking and nods at me.

"Excuse me for interrupting. I was wondering: our economics professor just explained to us why economics is a required subject and what the value of it is for the work we do. Could you do the same for psychology?"

He glares at me. "What an enormous animosity and aggression is hidden behind that question! You obviously have had bad experiences with psychologists in the past."

I'm shocked into silence and he continues his story where he left off. Afterwards a few people come up to me, praising my

CHAPTER 3 - THE WOMAN

speaking out.

"I was just asking a simple question," I mutter. "I don't know why he jumped all over me!"

A single mother standing nearby, who has already stated that raising children should be counted as work experience, sniffs, "You're obviously one of those people who knows all the answers!"

The contempt in her words slices through me. I turn away, ignoring her, and start talking to my friends from Haarlem.

My mother comes over to be with me when I'm expecting my first baby. As I lie on my bed, writhing with birthing pains, I feel her hand rubbing my lower back. My skin is on fire and I am conscious of only one thing: pain. Even the soft touch hurts.

"Don't touch me!" I snap.

She moves back and apologizes, "I thought that might make you feel better."

"I need to be alone." I turn my face to the wall.

In the neighborhood information center we have started in an abandoned shop front, I receive visitors and explain the new renovation plans to them, informing them of their position and their rights as homeowners or tenants. My two-year-old son, Hugo, sits at a table in the corner, his tow-headed curls bent over a drawing in fierce concentration. I stop for a moment to see what he has made.

"Look at this!" I exclaim to the other volunteer. "He's drawn a complete circle! That's such a huge step in the development of his brain!" I stroke his hair proudly and straighten his blue and white striped Osh-Kosh overalls. He beams at me with bright blue eyes.

Verdandi studies the fabric on her loom and shakes her head. "This woman has so much to learn," she mutters.

Urd smiles and reaches out to pluck thistles and sharp grasses to add to the thread rolling off her spindle. "She thinks she has finally arrived. She is just beginning her journey!"

Ten of us are gathered around in comfortable, plush armchairs or on the thick, blue Persian carpet. The group leader of this week of 'Games' gives us our next assignment.

"The one to start picks a person in the group and describes this person as a book, a movie or a flower. Then that person picks the next person." He looks around the group, smiling encouragingly.

A sickening feeling arises in my stomach. What if no one picks me? What if I'm the last one left and the person who has me doesn't know what to say about me? None of these people know me! This isn't fun! When I signed up for the Games Week at the *Volkshogeschool*[2] in beautiful, wooded Bergen, I imagined a fun holiday with new people. It's turning into a nightmare.

A woman starts and I hear others described as roses or beautiful books and movies. The describing game moves around the room and still no one has picked me. An hour later there are only two of us left.

I get to my feet. "Sorry, but I'm not feeling well. I'm going to bed early." I make my way from the room on unsteady legs and walk to my bedroom in the dormitory. I sit down on the edge of the narrow bed and try to control the turmoil in my head. It feels like anger. I don't understand why I should feel angry. Finally, I slide under the thin blanket, open a book, and start reading.

---

[2] An adult education school based on the ideas of the 19th century Danish philosopher Grundtvig.

CHAPTER 3 - THE WOMAN

A knock sounds on the door and I call out, "It's open."

The group leader enters the room and sits down on the edge of the bed near my feet. "How are you feeling?" He scrutinizes my face.

I glance up, briefly. "Oh, I'm fine. Just didn't feel well, that's all."

He places his hand on the blanket covering my leg. "I get the sense that you must have had to fight a lot when you were small." His eyes never leave my face.

The tears come suddenly, unexpectedly. My heart feels vulnerable, open and bleeding. I stare at him as the tears roll down my cheeks, unable to talk.

He continues to pat my leg. "It's okay, let yourself cry."

Slowly the tears subside. He looks at me questioningly. "Are you good now?"

"Yes," I say sniffing. "Do you have a Kleenex?"

The trainer hands me a tissue and stands up. "Good night, see you in the morning." The door closes gently behind him.

The rest of the week, I am careful to only join games that make me feel comfortable.

When I get home, I discuss the week with a girlfriend.

"I know there's all kinds of ugly stuff down inside me from my past. I'm sure I'm suppressing something. People seem to see me as someone totally different than how I see myself. I'm really shy. Why do people think I'm arrogant? But I don't want to do anything with this. It would be like opening Pandora's box. All that ugliness would come out and I don't think I can get the lid back on."

My friend gives me a quick hug. "You're better than you think you are. Stop worrying about what other people think of you."

I whimper and sob in my sleep, lost in my dreams, my body curled up in on itself, turned away from my husband's sleeping body.

I'm lost in a dark wood. Moonlight shimmers on rustling leaves.
A dark pile of brush conceals the witch but her bright eyes gleam.
I know that I have to go to the witch, even if it terrifies me.

Hunger

The local politician smiles at me warmly. "I like what you're saying and I like the way you express yourself. You have an amazing grasp of the Dutch language for someone who has only lived here for a few years."

I feel a warm glow building in my chest and smile back at him.

"Have you ever thought of going into politics? I've seen you leading these citizen participation evenings and you have a natural knack for leadership."

"Oh, I'm way too inexperienced for anything like that."

"Don't put yourself down, you speak straight from the heart. And that means you're speaking for the people. We need representatives like you, we're being governed by aristocrats with no sensitivity for what the people really want."

The glow spreads through my entire body. *Yes, I can do this!* I see myself orating before full rooms, confounding my opponents, bringing prosperity to the inner-city neighborhoods, and creating a world filled with peace and equality for all.

The party at the Zandvoort beach bar is in full swing. My husband, tucked into a corner of the full room, stares morosely into his beer glass and waves to the bartender for another. An older man is sitting next to him, talking nonstop and I see Anco's head nod occasionally. Large windows overlook the beach. Through the darkness outside, we vaguely see the white caps of waves coming in gently at low tide. My countless glasses of red wine have put a sparkle in my eye and loosened my tongue. I smile brilliantly at the handsome man standing in front of me, who is

CHAPTER 3 - THE WOMAN

giving me a tantalizing grin. I can't hear a word he's saying and the noise of all the chattering people hurts my head. My admirer and I slip away from the crowd and make our way down the beach towards the shallow water, our arms around each other, giggling nervously.

At the water's edge he challenges me. "Let's take off our clothes and go swimming. We can make love in the waves. I want you."

I look back at the beach-bar nervously. Can we be seen from there? I hedge and kiss him, trying to distract him.

"This is our only chance!" he urges, "Either you come into the water with me now or nothing is going to happen between us!"

I imagine myself lying in the water with him, waves coming in over on top of me, filling my nose and mouth. I shudder and suddenly feel quite sober. I turn and make my way back to the beach party, not even looking to see if he's following me. I push my way through the crowd and find my husband, looking bored and gloomy.

"Come on, let's go."

He gets up and follows me out.

I have just turned 30 and am two months pregnant with my second child. After a rocky period of indecision, I've started doing my best to keep my marriage from falling apart. We decide to do a road trip through the States with now four-year-old Hugo. I think it would a great idea to stop at my old college in Ohio and to meet up with Sam, whom I haven't seen in 10 years.

Sam is divorced from his first wife, and has come back to Ohio. His career as an artist fizzled out but he has trained himself as a master carpenter and furniture maker and is proud of his life as an artisan.

We take one look at each other and fall in love all over again. We steal away and talk, nonstop, for an entire night, the moonlight pouring in through the window.

"I remember how you stood naked, in front of the window, reached up, pulled down the moon, and handed it to me." He strokes my face and gazes into my eyes.

In the candid light of the early morning we decide not to act on our feelings. I need a chance to raise my children in a stable family setting. I go back to the Netherlands.

The midwife eyes me disapprovingly. "You only have two centimeters of dilation. Now stop trying to force things. The baby isn't due for another two weeks."

"I know you've been saying that," I sigh wearily. "But I'm sure the baby is coming tonight. I've been trying to tell you for weeks that it's going to be the middle of January, not the end!"

Her voice turns sharp. "I know what I'm doing. And you'd be better off relaxing and trying to enjoy the next two weeks. You know how to reach me if anything happens." She leaves, making her way down the creaky staircase and out the door.

That evening Anco takes me to a vernissage in a nearby art gallery, to distract me. We walk down the snow-covered street, gradually filling up with art galleries, small businesses, and renovated homes. As we push open the door to the gallery, bright light and loud music bombard my senses. Our host sweeps us both up in his huge arms and booms out a welcome. I try to find a place to sit and watch the guests, dressed in the latest avant-garde, artistic styles. The party bores me, the light hurts my eyes, I don't care for the art, and the chatter feels superficial. Suddenly I feel warm fluid trickling down my legs. Happy that I'm wearing a long dress, I turn and grab my husband's arm.

"We need to go home. NOW!"

The next day I cradle my newly-born son in my arms as he suckles my breast. We call him Jamie, honoring my Scottish ancestors. His big brother leans over me to peer into his face. Hugo has grown up so fast! I want to savor this one slowly, not missing a single day of his life.

Anger

"Relationship therapy hasn't changed much between us." My voice is flat and lifeless. I lean back in the threadbare velour armchair and glower at my husband. In his face I see the constant apathy and indecision that wears my patience down. I no longer see the sensitivity in his eyes, I no longer feel proud of his boundless creativity and his endless patience with our two boys.

I'm tired and grumpy after a day of city council debates on futile issues. Disagreements between myself and my party occur more and more often and I have become thoroughly disillusioned with local politics. I'm looking forward to the end of my four-year term so I can step down and find a good job. My stipendium as a council member provides us with a small steady income but I'm sick of poverty. I also feel dissatisfied with the degree in community work I have earned after four years of commuting to The Hague. There was no challenge earning the degree, I want to study something that engages my mind.

Anco shifts his feet and clears his throat. "Well, the therapist wasn't trying very hard, don't you think?"

"The therapist? We're the ones who are supposed to be working at this, don't blame her!" My voice rises and he shushes me, pointing up to the attic where the children are sleeping.

I ignore him and continue, "You haven't taken on a commercial photography project in years! I'm supporting you and the children and when I arrange a job for you, you ignore it! The house is as much of a mess as it was when we moved in! It's a health hazard and we're raising kids in it!"

He shrugs. "Ah well, I'm just not as ambitious as you are."

My anger floods me like a wave. My hand is clenching a half-filled glass coffee cup. Before I understand what I'm doing, I hurl it towards him, carefully aiming so it will barely miss him. It hits the wall behind him and the safety glass of the cup shatters. Brown coffee drips down the white, stucco surface. I get up, grab my handbag and run down the stairs, slamming the door as I leave.

Several months later, the divorce papers are filed. We manage to negotiate co-parenting and I move into my new flat.

The three-bedroom rental flat is on the third floor of a long, concrete housing block in a dreary 1960s neighborhood. I fill it with Ikea furniture and promise myself it's only a temporary solution. I find a job with a nearby town, working with citizen participation groups and urban development. I sign up to study public law at the University of Amsterdam. My employers are happy with me, I have adjusted to a schedule of days with, and days without, the children, and my social life is invigorating and fun.

Mummy sends me a long letter when she hears of the divorce.

Sometimes I wonder if there is something terribly wrong with us, she writes. *Something that inhibits us from finding or holding on to love. Maybe you inherited it from me.*

SYMBIOSIS
The local pub doesn't start filling up until around 11 in the evening. The room is filled with cigarette smoke and chatter. I'm leaning against the burnished wooden bar, relaxing with friends, and enjoying my evening off. I'm feeling contented, even though the cigarette smoke irritates my eyes and the noise hurts my ears.

I've just started to think about leaving, when the door opens and closes again. A tall, dark-haired man with dark blue eyes walks in. He is, without doubt, the most beautiful man I have ever seen

CHAPTER 3 - THE WOMAN

in my life. Our eyes meet and I see his eyes widen. He walks past me and orders a beer at the bar. Then he goes to lean against a wall, never taking his eyes off me.

I start feeling uneasy. He's too good to be true. I'm sure he must be some kind of a crank. But I'm fascinated at the same time. I take my beer and walk over to him.

"Hi, I'm Madeleine," I beam my most disarming smile at him.

"I'm Piet. Pleased to meet you." His voice is deep and slightly hesitant, as if he isn't accustomed to talking much.

I toss my curls and my little turquoise earrings bob back and forth. "What do you want?"

A smile breaks his face wide open. "I want to be in love with someone for the rest of my life."

The sun starts shining through a curtain in my head and I suddenly realize I have lived in the dark my entire life.

Dusk is falling in the *Haarlemmer Hout*. As we walk beneath the ancient trees of this wooded park, the air is filled with birdsong. As if every bird in the world has gathered here to pour out his song of love into the universe. We walk hand in hand, without speaking, surrounded by May magic. The evening stroll seems to last an eternity.

We buy a large, romantic house in a peaceful area of Haarlem. Built in the 1930s, the brick walls are set off by green and white, carved wood trim. Inside, a turning staircase is illuminated by a large stained glass window in the stairwell. The fencing of the front garden is covered with pink roses and the large, deep, back garden is filled with trees, wildflowers, and a winding path to a stone circle in back.

The children have their own rooms and a separate playroom. As they grow older, they start bicycling back and forth from their father's house to ours. Jamie takes to his new step-father immediately. Between Piet and Hugo, however, is some tension I try not to see.

"Hugo's not feeling happy at the new secondary school. It's so huge, I think he feels lost there. I might switch him to a smaller one, so he's under less pressure."

"He could try harder," Piet snorts. "He spends a lot of his time fooling around and doesn't take school very seriously."

My love is a vegetarian and a sportsman. I adjust my diet to his and take up running and yoga. I even start playing the violin again. It feels as if I have finally proven to myself and to my parents that I can be successful at anything and everything I do.

Friends consider us the perfect couple. We never argue and do everything together. He has a good job working for the airlines and we fly back and forth to the States, usually to run marathons. Often we use the trips to visit my family. My mother becomes quite enamored of this new love in my life… my knight on a white horse.

Mummy starts making frequent trips to come and stay with us.

"I love it here. I love being with you. I'm so happy that you live here, I just wish I could come more often."

At 60 she still looks 40. We go clothes shopping together, arm in arm, and the shopkeeper thinks we're sisters.

The intimacy between us increases and she starts confessing her secrets to me: an illicit love affair, endless flirtations, disillusionment in her marriage, a sense that she hasn't made anything useful out of her life.

"Why don't you leave him? You two fight all the time, it makes me miserable to witness it and I know the others feel the same way."

She sighs and takes another sip of her coffee. "I couldn't face a second divorce. Besides, how would I live? I would be all alone

CHAPTER 3 - THE WOMAN

and I wouldn't be able to afford to come over and see you and the boys anymore."

I frown slightly and then drop the subject. The idea of staying in a marriage that isn't working sounds impossible to me. But the thought of my mother never being able to travel again seems almost impossible too.

On Saturday mornings we enjoy walking downtown to do our weekly grocery shopping: cheese at the cheese-shop, vegetables at the greengrocer, bread at the bakery, and a stop at the organic food-store on the way home. This morning, eight-year-old Jamie accompanies us, slipping his hand into mine as we walk along. Piet frowns.

"You're not a baby anymore, Jamie. You can walk on your own."

Jamie and I drop hands. He looks as unhappy as I feel, but I tell myself Piet is probably right, I coddle the child too much.

Piet and I shoulder our backpacks, wave goodbye to our hosts at the lovely old inn outside of King's Stanley and set out again on the trail. We've been walking the Cotswold Way for six days now, drinking in the peaceful English landscape, spread out beneath our feet from the high escarpment of the Cotswold Hills. A few hours later, we enter bluebell-carpeted Standish Woods. I love walking. Every flower, every tree, every feather on the ground, every bird-filled hedgerow is here to savor slowly. The hectic drive of my work in urban development, the distractions of children, school, activities, daily life... all this falls away and I am one with the land.

A week later we arrive at the end of the trail in Chipping Camden. A taxi takes us back to Bath so we can catch the train to Heathrow Airport. The taxi speeds past familiar landmarks, covering the distance we took almost two weeks to traverse, in a half hour.

Each summer we pack up the tent and pile the children into the car, driving down to Bretagne, the Dordogne, or Provence for weeks of camping, fishing, canoeing and simply exploring nature. Sometimes we go on rambles with the boys: with 15-year-old Hugo we walk through Wales, carrying tents on our backs. A few years later, we traipse through the Spanish Pyrenees with 14-year-old Jamie.

LYRICAL
A stiff wind is battering the heavy brown canvas sails of the *Leonora* as we make our way down the Old Maas from Rotterdam. We're heading towards the shelter of the *Biesbosch*, the marshy wetland area of the Netherlands. Each summer we take a week off to go sailing in the old flat-bottomed sailboat that belongs to Piet's family. With its sideboards and heavy ropes, it's a boat for brawny men. But I love the freedom of being out on the water.

I've gone up to sit in the bow, enjoying the wind blowing through my hair and spying out birds with my camera, when Piet shouts out to me.

"We have to take down the mast, we're too tall to go under the railroad bridge!"

"How can we do that? We're almost there!" A feeling of panic overtakes me.

"You take the rudder, I'm going forward. Keep the bow heading into the wind!" he shouts back.

I can do this, I tell myself. I hold the long wooden rudder with both hands and watch anxiously as Piet furls the sails and then loosens the bolts holding the mast into place, slowly letting it descend onto the boom support. I start the engine.

A few hours later we have arrived in the calm waters of the Biesbosch, sheltered by reeds and willow trees. We toss out

CHAPTER 3 - THE WOMAN

the anchor, coil the ropes, and open up the small cabin. Then we uncork a bottle of wine and lean back. The water rocks the boat gently; a beaver swims by, only its head and a v-shaped wake visible above the mirror of water. Crested grebes dive deep down to the bottom of the marsh, resurfacing minutes later. The only sound is the cheeping of the little black-and-white coots, as they swim with their offspring, tiny balls of ruddy fuzz, trailing behind them. I never sleep as soundly as when I'm on the boat.

A small crowd of people has gathered for the summer evening recital. At first I ignore them, focusing all my attention on my instrument, tightening the long flexible bow, adjusting the shoulder rest. I walk over to the piano where my music partner sounds an A. I play soft chords, turning the smooth black tuning-pegs until my critical ear is satisfied.

Then I finally face the audience. I skim their expectant faces, trained by years of working in a public function to feel comfortable in front of a group.

"Thank you for coming. We're going to play Faure's *Sicilienne*. One of my favorite pieces." I ignore the sheet music on the stand nearby, it's there in case I freeze. But I won't.

I bring my attention to the ground beneath my feet, poise my bow above the waiting violin, and listen to the opening piano notes. Then I take a deep breath and gently touch the strings, breathing into the music. The music, my body, and the instrument move in unison. I sway, riding the notes like a surfer cresting waves. I coax the soul of the song from the strings... come to me, let me sing you! I love this lyrical style and it suits me. I offer the song to the world, oblivious to the people in the room.

It's over way too quickly. I lower my violin and turn to smile at my piano partner. Then I turn to the room, bowing to the applause that has broken out.

The mortar and pestle land with a huge splash in the water. The mermaid doesn't even turn to look but starts laughing.

"Welcome Baba Yaga! I was wondering when you would show up!"

Fierce brown eyes glare over the edge of the precariously rocking mortar. "How can you stand living in the water all the time!" The witch pulls herself up carefully and uses her broom to keep her balance. "We have to talk about this human of ours. She's living an illusion!"

"She needs this illusion now, she needs to feel safe and loved. She felt unsafe for so long." The mermaid's eyes are sad and she traces circles with her hand in the choppy, grey-green water.

"Well, it's time she woke up! Or she will live out a lifetime without ever finding out who she is."

The mermaid nods, "I think she's strong enough now to take the next step."

Urd's eyes twinkle as she starts collecting thorny rose bushes and thistles to spin into her thread.

The rune this time is ᚺ Hagalaz: Disruption.

CHAPTER 3 - THE WOMAN

Cracks in the ice

I'm flying through the dark on the back of a huge male presence. Way below me, mountains, rivers, and cities rush by. The Being points out places I have visited, milestones in my life. As we soar through the dark, I feel at one with him. A rush of joy fills me.

When I wake up, I feel a twinge of guilt. I don't tell my husband about the dream.

I am Superwoman. I juggle mothering, college classes, and a full time job. I take the boys to their music and sport lessons and help them with their homework. At work, I make one promotion after the other, praised by all for my sense of purpose and responsibility, my talent for people management, and my creativity. I'm proud of my trim, athletic body and my heart flutters whenever a man makes me a compliment. My husband adores me. My life is perfect.

And now I'm sitting next to a hospital bed and all this falls away and becomes meaningless. My vision and perception is funneled into one object, one object only. I watch my firstborn son's breath lift his chest gently and let it fall, I count the breaths. Trying not to see the tubes connected to his arm, pouring antibiotics and painkillers into his body. Trying not to see the nasal tube keeping him hydrated.

The day before, Hugo called me from his rooms, where he'd been living since he left home at 18, two years earlier. I've been doing my best not to play the over-solicitous mother. I was happy to hear him, until he told me his news.

"Mom, I'm really sick and the doctor has sent for the ambulance."

Will he live? He *will* live! I refuse to consider any other possibility and fix fierce eyes on him, willing him to get better. His eyes flutter open and he grins weakly.

"That methadone isn't half bad!' he jokes.

I smile and let my hand rest gently on his leg.

"At least you don't feel the pain."

His eyes close again. His young body looks so incongruous against the white sheets and sterile ward, the beds filled with old men breathing laboriously. His hair falls in long dirty-blond dreadlocks on the pillow and his tattoos are black against his sallow skin. His body is wracked by the infections in his abdominal cavity, caused by a burst appendix that wasn't attended to fast enough.

Nurses start busying themselves, lifting his body to wash him, checking the racks with bottles that surround him, taking his temperature. I can't stay here permanently, I'll only get in the way. I don't know where to go so I decide to go home. The nurses give me a beeper and promise to let me know if any changes occur. I'm back a few hours later. Nothing matters any more, nothing but my son, fighting for his life in a hospital bed.

As the months pass and the danger decreases, I find some semblance of balance, dividing my attention between the hospital, Piet, Jamie, and my work. In the hospital, Hugo shuffles up and down the hallway on legs like sticks, pushing a rack on wheels with his IV bottles. I pour my energy into organizing a private room for him, away from all the dying old men, and bringing him treats he's allowed to eat.

When he finally comes home, I try to pick up the old thread of my life. But something has shifted inside me. The first crack in the ice of my perfect life has appeared.

CHAPTER 3 - THE WOMAN

My mother is turning 70 and she has come to spend the Christmas holidays with me and my family. We attend a concert in the Amsterdam *Concertgebouw*. Bartók's *Concerto for Orchestra* is on the program. Mummy's eyes are rapt and her hands clasped in front of her chest. At one point she leans towards me and whispers, "Can you hear the world crying?"

My husband is out for the evening and Mummy is sitting on a floor cushion at my feet, leaning against my knees, as we share a bottle of good red wine. She takes a deep breath and starts talking.

"There's something I need to tell you. You need to know this before something happens to me and my secret dies with me." She starts telling me the story of the long trip by freighter to China to make a documentary movie, her love affair with the Norwegian cameraman, and the ensuing pregnancy.

"So my first husband is not your father, the Norwegian is."

I'm stunned. But the story makes sense and many tiny details I had never understood before fall into place. "Who else knows this?"

"No one. I never told anyone about it, not even my mother and sisters. You *must* keep this a secret!" Her green eyes gaze up at me, fear and shame shining out of them.

My only thought is, *oh my god, another secret!* I don't understand her secrets. I hate secrets, I want to be open and transparent, as transparent as glass. I promise her I will tell no one in the States. But my children and husband have a right to know. She writes down my father's name for me on a slip of paper and I tuck it away where I won't lose it.

The next morning she goes up to my husband when she comes down for breakfast. "Do you despise me now?" She gazes up into his eyes.

He smiles gently and takes her into his arms. "Of course not."

I'm seated across from my superior. He pushes his chair back slightly and eases back, his paunch stretching the buttons on his yellow and black checked shirt. Eyes narrowed, watching me trying to take in what he's telling me. The environmental affairs department I have led for the past three years will not survive this latest reorganization. It will be split up and the personnel will be divided among other departments. There is no management position for me in the new organization. I will be offered a position as project manager.

I lean forward and place my forearms on his desk, challenging him.

"Why are they doing this?" I know my question is futile. "I have explained over and over how important it is to keep this team together. We've been so successful at implementing new procedures and systems. You know we have!"

His eyes are cold. "I guess you didn't explain it to the right people. It doesn't always matter if you're right or not. It's about making sure the people in power support you."

I push my chair back, suddenly feeling my heart pound and my cheeks flare. "Well, thanks for your support!" I grab my things and leave the room.

I tell my secretary what happened and that I'm going home for the afternoon. At home, I open a bottle of 1987 *Chambolle-Musigny* from our cellar, put Mahler's *Kindertotenlieder* on the CD player, and start to cry. By the time Piet comes home from work, the bottle is empty and I'm curled up on the couch, clutching a pillow to my belly, face caked with salt tears.

SHARK

René, our energetic, blond coach looks around the circle at each of us. She smiles brightly and turns to her flipchart. To compensate for the loss of my position, I've been sent to a Management Development Program. A year of coaching, lectures, and experiential learning will help me to develop the management skills I need.

"Today we're going to talk about defense mechanisms. Basically you can categorize people as Sharks, Carp, or Dolphins. When Sharks feel threatened, they know that attacking is their best defense. Carp, on the other hand, will escape by diving deep down to hide from the threat. And then you have the Dolphins, who have learned to rise playfully above the threat and solve the problem."

As I listen, I feel positive that I'm a Carp. Every threatening situation sends me into a dizzy spell of avoidance. She hands out a test and we fill in the questions diligently. I'm astounded by the results: I score very high as a Shark.

Seated at the pinewood dining-room table at home, I pull a set of colored pencils towards me and open the new black leather-bound notebook. Painstakingly, I draw a huge spreading tree with strong limbs and deep roots. The upper branches sway in the wind and the leaves are open to sunlight. Birds perch on the branches. The roots are large and extend deeply into the ground, anchoring the tree and drawing up nourishment. The tree is a visual metaphor for the transformation I wish to go through during the program. I wish to become as strongly rooted and welcoming as this tree.

The front door opens and closes. I get up and run to the hall, into Piet's open arms. He puts down his briefcase and follows me into the room, where I show him my drawing, chattering happily.

"I've been thinking about my work." I clasp his arm eagerly. "I've let myself be led by what they want, climbing up and up in the hierarchy because I feel flattered by the recognition I get.

But am I doing what I really want? What I really want is to make a difference in the world... or the town... or in people's lives. Not just grow higher and higher until I reach the top. I get too caught up in other people's power-games. I want to get away from this organization and start somewhere fresh, find a job that allows me to really be a change agent!"

Piet looks at me searchingly. "You could try looking for another job."

"Part of this program entails doing interim management somewhere else for three months. That could give me the opportunity to move on. One of the interim spots is in Utrecht. I might try for that "

He frowns. "That's an hour away by train. Isn't that too long a commute?"

"I can try it for those three months and see. There may not be a permanent position open there anyway." I shrug and get up to prepare dinner. I'll cope. I always do.

Utrecht feels like a brand new world. A large government body, caught up in the challenge of becoming a learning organization. Unencumbered by how my colleagues expect me to act, I try out new concepts and ways of communicating with people. I meet a woman who is starting a new project management agency within the city's organization. I like what she's doing and she likes my work. She's looking for people like me to come strengthen her agency.

The coaching at the Management Development Program continues, helping us integrate our newly-found skills into our lives.

"We had the most fantastic lecturer today!" My words tumble over each other in my enthusiasm. I rattle on and on, not seeing how his eyes start glazing over. "... Present-day society inhibits this development. The society that goes with this stage of

CHAPTER 3 - THE WOMAN

development is governed by true communication on all levels. Remember how we used to believe in the Age of Aquarius? That's the next step for society!"

Piet sits back and gazes at me, pensively. "That is the most ridiculous thing I've ever heard."

I feel myself becoming very small and retreating into a long dark tunnel. Piet excuses himself to go to the kitchen and prepare dinner. I open a book and start reading.

THE FALL

At my new job as a project manager in Utrecht, I meet a man who doesn't think my ideas are ridiculous at all. We grow close.

One night Adam finally said, it was the snake or him, Eve was going to have to choose. She gazed at him with huge eyes and, as she struggled to understand, she thought of the apple tree and the luscious, unreasonably forbidden, fruit. A voice inside her tickled in her head, "I am a free person with a free will!" She got out of bed, marched out to the apple tree, grabbed a big juicy apple and took a huge bite. The apple was delicious. But as she ate, she gazed around at her garden and saw it grow smaller and smaller and recede further and further away. The colors faded and went to grey. The world around her started growing dark.

The voice in her head said, "You can't go back". She panicked and turned to the snake, but he just laughed at her.

"You're an adult woman," he said, "try to behave like one."

We lie next to each other in the dark, in the double bed we have slept in for the past 12 years. Both of us lie on our backs, sleepless in spite of the exhaustion that has overtaken us after two weeks of constant discussions, tears, and accusations.

"Do you love him?" Piet's voice sounds resigned.

I turn towards him, "No! I already told you, I have stopped seeing him. This isn't about him, it's about us!"

His voice turns rough with tears. "What do you want?"

"I want us to do this relationship therapy. I want to understand what's going on!"

He sighs. "It doesn't make sense to go into therapy if you can't promise me that you're committed to stay and make this work."

"I only want to understand what's happening between us." I turn away. "When I try to imagine the future, all I see is an empty white space, filled with calm, where I can be at peace."

He falls silent. Then his voice sounds again, louder this time. "Well, if that's the way you feel, then I guess you should leave."

I step out of bed, open the white louvre doors of the wall-to-wall closet, and start packing my bags.

"That was not courageous! She's running away!" Urd's voice is low and full of fury.

Verdandi stops weaving and strokes the web thoughtfully. "That's the trouble with free will. Humans sometimes take the wrong path for all the wrong reasons."

Skuld pushes back her veil, showing a haggard, white face. Her eyes are as cold as winter. She pulls out her knife and carves Isa: *danger, on the tree bark.*

The lush green lawn in front of the stone cottage in Herefordshire is filled with wide-spreading trees, the kind of tree you only find

CHAPTER 3 - THE WOMAN

on the English countryside with its stone walls, rolling fields, and grazing cattle. My eyes don't see the pastoral scene, instead a sense of being utterly lost engulfs me. Piet has moved on with his life and has fathered a child by another woman. The man I had turned to for comfort just laughed and turned away. I've been exiled from Paradise by my own doing. I can never go back again. I'm so ashamed, I've failed at another marriage. What is wrong with me?

Sobs start coming up from somewhere deep inside me. Marriage gave me a sense of identity. Now I'm lost, drowning in my own tears, gulping for air. I no longer understand who I am or what my life is about. My boys and my job are the only thing that keep me functioning normally.

My sister Annie and her two toddlers emerge from the cottage that we've rented together for the holiday week. I can't stand the thought of being sociable and go inside and upstairs to my bed.

My mother enters the room, I sense her sit down next to me.

"What's the matter?" She lays a hand on my back.

"I miss him so much!" I sob.

"Isn't it a bit late for that now? You should have thought of that earlier."

I turn away on my side, letting her hand fall away. She gets up and silently leaves the room.

The psychologist's eyes watch me thoughtfully through his wire-rimmed glasses. His voice is calming, avuncular.

"I studied your test results. There's really nothing wrong with you except the fact that you're extremely sensitive."

I gaze back at him numbly, trying to make sense of what he's saying.

He continues, "I think we should focus this therapy on teaching you to balance your rational, thinking self, which is very strongly developed, with your emotional self, which tends to take over at times. It seems to be either one or the other, they don't work together very well."

"I guess that makes sense," I say hesitantly.

In the months that follow, he helps me examine the beliefs I have grown up with, the need to achieve and prove myself, the yearning to be loved. I keep looking for love, for the ideal relationship, instead of learning to give myself the love I yearn for.

Step by step, I start living my own life. I put aside all activities that feel as though I am doing them to impress other people or earn approval, including my violin. But something closes down inside me. I don't want to have my heart broken, not ever again.

WRONG MAN, RIGHT PLACE

I walk up the six steps to the front door of my canal-side home in Utrecht. I own the high-ceilinged, stately ground floor and the basement floor with a small walled garden at its back. This is the first home that is truly mine and I have lavished all my creativity and energy into making it a beautiful place where I can be myself. I love the soft peach walls, the bronze-colored raw silk floor-length curtains and the 10-foot ornamental ceiling. But when I walk through the door in the evening, after a challenging, busy day, managing complex urban projects and working with people, I close the bustle of the city and its people out and spend my evenings surfing the Internet.

As I start putting groceries away, the phone rings. I sigh and answer it. Franz's eager voice is at the other end, just as I expected. He has an uncanny sense of knowing when I arrive home.

"Hi babe, how was your day?"

I mumble something noncommittal and he continues with a

CHAPTER 3 - THE WOMAN

long story about his own day. I tuck the phone between my ear and shoulder and continue putting things away, preparing dinner, picking up things in the house.

An hour later, I finally say. "Hey Franz, I need to eat my dinner before it gets cold. I'll be online after I've eaten. See you then."

My ear is red and warm from the phone call. I eat my dinner in silence.

A friend asks me what I see in this nine years younger, immature laborer with his shoulder-length black hair, beer belly, and bad temper.

I shrug my shoulders. "He's good company. It's better than being alone. And besides, he's part Indonesian and a great cook!"

A year later he has convinced me to move down to the south of the country, closer to where he works, so we can live together, we and his two big dogs. I'm sorry to leave my beautiful home and I stipulate that I want a house out in the countryside this time. I'm sick of living in the city.

I steer the car slowly and nervously along the narrow dike and down the steep driveway. The real estate man has already arrived and is talking with the owners. The house is small but it has a large free-standing garage that could be converted into a guesthouse and workspace. Still feeling very shaky about the driveway, I let them escort me inside. The first thing I see is a wall of little square windowpanes, opening up the eastern side of the living room onto a view of fields and sky. To the south, French doors open out onto a huge, lush garden filled with beautiful trees and flowering shrubs. I fall in love immediately.

And so I come to Brabant, very close to my beloved *Biesbosch*. I commute to work in Utrecht, braving the rush-hour traffic. I love my work and, as time progresses, I start coaching and training younger colleagues, teaching them that project management is more about working with people than simply sticking to time and budget constraints. When I arrive home in the evening, the pressures of work slide away from me as I gaze out at hawks and harriers soaring high above the fields. And I try to ignore the fact that Franz starts drinking beer steadily when he gets home from work and ends up snoring on the couch in front of the television.

Mummy comes to the Netherlands one more time. We sit comfortably in large leather armchairs, drinking *Hertog Jan* ale from the bottle. She carefully peels the label off the bottle and pastes it onto a piece of paper.

"All these people who say that they love and admire me," she says, morosely studying her handiwork, "If any of them ever knew who I really am, they wouldn't love me anymore."

I study her once beautiful face, now worn down by unhappiness and guilt, and ravaged by Parkinson's Disease. Always looking for love and never finding it. I see myself in this, I too have been searching for love my entire life. I get up and hug her, "I know more about you than most people do. And I love you dearly."

As Parkinson's continues to attack my mother's body and mind, my sister Annie and her husband decide to take on the roles of caregivers. The house in Westport is sold and my parents move into a new wing built onto their large house in New Jersey. I start traveling to the States twice a year, to see as much of my mother as possible and to give Annie some moral support.

A *FATHER*
I read and reread the letter in my hands, the carefully spelled

CHAPTER 3 - THE WOMAN

English and neat handwriting.

"I believe you think I am your father. I hope you are right. Your mother never wanted to talk about this and I had no way of knowing."

Warmth builds up in my heart and spreads to all parts of my body. I have a father! And he likes the idea!

A few months later I emerge into the Arrivals Hall at Oslo's Gardermoen Airport. He smiles and waves. I walk quickly up to him and we embrace.

"Oh my goodness, you're so tall!" I gaze up at him.

In spite of his 80 years, Njørd towers over me. His iron-grey hair is combed carefully to the side. Large blue eyes gaze at me behind thick, black-rimmed glasses.

He introduces me to his daughter, Jorunn, a slim, blond woman with a warm, welcoming smile.

We drive to his tiny one-bedroom home, the kind of house that Norway provides for its pensioners. We perch on Scandinavian wooden furniture and Jorunn busies herself in the kitchen, making coffee. He leans back and studies me shyly.

"You must ask me questions. I'm not good at this. I'm not accustomed to talking about myself."

I ply him with questions about his life and how he met my mother.

"I was a cameraman for Ingmar Bergman for several years. Then I decided to go to New York and find work there. Your mother and her husband were really just artists, dabbling in movie making. And, of course, I had a lot of experience. They wanted to make a documentary about the changes in China. So, when they found a sponsor, they hired me to come with them."

He continues, searching for the proper English words, searching his memory for the details.

"In those days, movie equipment was very heavy and bulky. We loaded it all onto a freighter and started the long trip down, from New York, through the Panama Canal, towards Manila. I did some shoots on the way and your mother helped me, changing the large cassettes. She was very unhappy and we grew close."

I lean towards him, listening attentively, entranced at hearing the story properly for the first time.

"And then your mother announced she was pregnant. But she drew back from us both and refused to talk about it. I think she was frightened, or maybe ashamed.

When we got to Manila, there was a telegram waiting from the sponsor, saying that Mao had started to march on Beijing and it was too dangerous to continue on to China. The sponsor ordered your mother and her husband back to New York. I traveled up to Tokyo before returning. Then I heard that your mother had gone to her mother's home in Connecticut with the baby… with you. I never saw her again."

He goes on to relate how he returned to Norway afterwards and became a film director, producer, and screenplay writer. He speaks candidly of his two failed marriages and his ongoing battle against alcoholism.

I pull out a photograph of my mother to show him. He studies it carefully.

"I'm afraid I don't recognize her. I no longer remember what she looked like, I only remember that she was very beautiful and very brave."

My heart skips a beat and then continues to beat steadily. What did I expect? That he sees her photo after 55 years and exclaims, "This is she! The woman I never stopped loving!"? It was just an affair, nothing more.

I repeat the words that night in my journal, *It was just an affair.*

CHAPTER 3 - THE WOMAN

The next day I meet handsome and self-assured Ragnar, my Norwegian brother. He laughs when he sees me and turns to his sister. "I was considering asking for a DNA test. After all, he is a well-known person in our country. But now that I see her, it's obvious!"

They both turn to me. "You look so much like him, it's uncanny. You have his eyes." My sister smiles warmly.

I feel welcomed. I have found a new family.

The wide branches of Ygdrassil hold many visitors, including a large white-tailed sea eagle. He looks up from cleaning his long black talons with his sharp yellow beak and surveys the mountains, fjords, and forests around him. Then he lets out a loud scream and flies off. Urd shields her eyes from the sun as she watches him disappear.

"When will she start discovering that anger is simply an expression of love?" She speaks out loud, more to herself than to her sisters, but Skuld pushes her veil back and answers her.

"I guess we need to lend her a hand there."

Skuld turns to the tree and carves the rune ᚢ Uruz: challenge, into the ash tree. Then, below, she carves ᛞ Dagaz or dawning.

CHOICES AND GOODBYES

Hugo, and I sit across from each other at a rickety little table on an Amsterdam sidewalk. We lift our beer glasses and clink them together. Then we dig into our salads. I finally pick up the courage to start.

"You asked how I am. Well, I'm thinking I made a big mistake by letting Franz into my life. He sucks all the energy out of me and I get nothing in return."

Hugo's eyes twinkle. "Jamie and I could never figure out what you saw in that guy! I was wondering when you'd come to your senses."

I shift my feet uncomfortably. "The funny thing is that I was never in love with him. But he seemed to be a good distraction. I guess I wasn't seeing things very clearly. Maybe I felt that I didn't deserve any better." I sigh and take a big gulp of beer. " I've made a big mess of things, I'm sorry I put you two through so much."

Hugo smiles at me and leans back. "You know, Mom, I'm a pretty happy guy. Even though I didn't finish college and am not really making anything spectacular out of my life. And you know why I'm capable of being happy? Because my entire life I have always known that, whatever I do – whether I succeed at things or make a mess of them – you will always accept me and love me as I am."

I gaze at him, stunned by his insight and the grace with which he shares this with me.

"You and your brother are the best things that ever happened to me," I whisper.

We hold hands for a few minutes and then finish our supper.

When I tell Franz to leave and take his dogs with him, he packs his things calmly and moves to Breda.

My office is a sunny room, high up on the eighth floor of the urban development tower, overlooking the western side of Utrecht. From my window I can see several major roads and intersections, all part of my responsibility as temporary manager of the Infrastructure Program. The town will be spending billions of euros to upgrade their infrastructure during the next five years and the manager has just left for another job. Reluctantly (I was trying to

CHAPTER 3 - THE WOMAN

get away from urban development projects and move towards facilitating organizational changes), I take the offer to stand in for several months until a new manager can be found. And, as the weeks go by, I find myself warming to the challenge. My team is made up of enthusiastic, capable individuals, hungry for proper leadership and buffeted by reorganizations. They are happy with my personal approach and my willingness to stand up for them.

A manager to whom I must answer during this temporary job is now standing in the doorway, while I hold my weekly meeting with my team. He's obviously waiting for me to drop everything and listen to him. I finally smile apologetically at the six people gathered around my small meeting table, and look up.

"Hi Thom, you needed to see me?" My voice is polite and my eyes hold the suggestion of a smile that he does not answer.

"There's an extra meeting on the budget cuts tomorrow morning at 7:30 in the alderman's office. I expect you to be there."

I frown, Friday is my day off and I will be meeting with fellow students from the counseling training I have recently started. "I'm sorry, I know the alderman is busy but you'll have to do it without me. I can't make it."

His voice hardens and he takes one step forward. No one ever says "no" to him. "You have to come! You'll just have to cancel whatever else it is you're doing."

I lean back, my eyes meeting his levelly. "I'm very sorry, but I can't make it."

He turns abruptly and walks away.

The witch laughs triumphantly and steers her mortar and pestle straight towards the waxing crescent moon. "She is finally beginning to understand! Hold your ground my girl! Feel how powerful you are!"

The country of my birth tugs at me. I don't understand why I am in this place filled with river clay, farmland, and tidy, practical people. I long for wild nature, and the comforting presence of forests. I long for something I cannot name, it eludes my grasp and I feel restless. I chase the restlessness away with long hours on the Internet, glasses of wine, and trips to the States. I need to put down roots somewhere.

And I do love the trees and flowers in my garden, the peaceful seclusion here, the awe-inspiring sunrises, and the roe deer wandering the fields. I've become an inspired photographer, recording all the breathtaking images of nature around my home. So where does this restlessness come from?

It's a sunny spring day when Annie calls and says that I have to come quickly. My mother doesn't have much time left. I drop everything and get on the next flight to Newark, New Jersey.

And here I am, sitting with her, her hand clutching my arm. There's not very much left of her, like an autumn leaf dried up so much that it will float away if you blow on it. She has retreated into a dark wood of dementia and hardly communicates with the outside world. But her body has once again rallied from a bladder infection and the hospice nurse has advised me not to wait around until she dies.

I start talking. I stroke her hand and tell her how much I love her.

Her eyes open and she starts crying. "I'm so sorry. I'm so very, very sorry!"

I tell her not to be sorry, to forgive herself, to let go and let herself go into the light.

I return to the Netherlands. A few months later, in the middle of the night, the phone call comes that she has passed peacefully.

CHAPTER 3 - THE WOMAN

As I dissolve with sobs, sitting in the dark, I feel her close, trying in vain to comfort me.

Soon after, the phone call arrives from Oslo that my father, Njørd, has also passed away. Though I do not go to Oslo for his funeral, still too overwhelmed by the death of my mother, Jorunn sends me a photograph of the wreath on the coffin. On the broad white ribbon, the names of his children are printed in silvery letters. The first name is Madeleine.

In October, my American family and I meet in Westport to bury my mother's ashes in the family plot. It is a beautiful autumn day, with blue skies and blazing colors, the season Mummy loved the most. We collect her favorite shells on Compo Beach, along with orange and scarlet leaves, and place them on the urn before closing the grave.

> *The mermaid sits on her rock, her hair glistening in the starlight. She casts out her nets and pulls in silvery fish. Then she throws out the nets again and lets the fish go. She sings a song of letting go and of acceptance.*

4

THE CRONE

Shifting focus

We sit on chairs in a circle with our eyes closed. Twelve aspiring counselors and our trainer. The room is filled with evocative, hauntingly beautiful music.

> *I am sitting at the end of a dock, looking out to sea. My feet dangle in the cool water. I hear the swish of waves lapping on the shore and the sound of seabirds calling. I am all alone and this fills me with a sense of sorrow and deep yearning. The thought crosses my mind that I am nearing the end of my life span. I don't want to grow old alone. I've failed at all my relationships, I'm wounded at the core. My anger has turned inwards, a slow burning rage that only eats away at myself. I'm lonely, restless, self-destructive, and unhappy.*

Our trainer, Nel, invites us to share our vision and thoughts. As I speak, I try to breathe through the tightness in my chest.

Nel looks at me with a shrewd smile. Her brown eyes speak of kindness and understanding. "What you need to realize, is that you're on your way to becoming a wise woman."

I frown at her words. "I'm anything but wise!"

"It's a question of shifting your perspective," she says gently. "Start to look at things from a different angle. Your life's experiences help you understand how other people struggle with their lives, their wounds, their relationships. You can view yourself as a failed old woman or you can turn this around and see yourself as a wise woman, searching your inner core for the wisdom to heal others."

As I gaze up at the star-filled sky, a soft voice starts whispering in my head. Is it The Witch speaking or The Mermaid? Or are they one and the same?

"Your grandmother lived alone, refusing to acknowledge her grief. Your mother lived with shame, in fear of being alone, in fear of losing love. You can turn everything that has happened to you, and to them, into a source of true strength. You don't need to be caught up in tragedy.

Even your core wound is a source of strength. Look at the centaur, Chiron. He needed to be mortally wounded by one of Hercules' poisoned arrows to become the great healer he was."

I stand in the large rectangular room, facing the mirror. I try not to look at myself. I look old in the fluorescent light and, besides, I need to focus on the QiGong teacher. This is my third year and I am still trying to do all the movements as accurately as possible. He has said countless times, "Just don't try so hard." But that makes no sense to me. And so I keep trying.

Now we're doing something deceptively simple. We stand and move one hand away and back in a circular motion, then the other, repeating this again and again.

"Think of it as casting a fishing net to bring in the *qi*," he suggests as he repeats the gesture.

I cast my net gently, hauling in tiny, silvery minnows of *qi*.

CHAPTER 4 - THE CRONE

Over and over again. And suddenly I feel it: currents of tingling electricity moving from my lower back through my body and out through my arms. As I continue casting my net, the currents move through my body, following the motion.

What is this? My rational mind has trouble accepting the conclusion: this must be the *qi*. At home, I lie in bed and feel the remains of the mysterious tingling lingering in my body. I decide that, if I can feel it, I'm going to have to accept that it exists. Even if I don't understand it. And, if I can direct it through my own body, I can also use it to heal others.

My manager and I seat ourselves at the round table in her office for my yearly evaluation. As she starts shuffling in her papers, I take the lead.

"There's something I should tell you before we start in on the routine stuff. As you know, during the last couple of years, I have derived the most pleasure in my work from coaching and training colleagues. This is why I decided to go back to school: to train as a counselor and open my own practice."

She nods. "I can't deny you've been invaluable in that sense and the project management training you developed has now become a product our clients ask for."

"I think that's wonderful!" I continue. "And I love this agency, I love the comradeship and the way you allow us to work independently and support us. But I also think it's time I left."

Her eyes widen but she waits for me to continue.

"I have a few years to go before I reach retirement age. I could stay and wait until then. But it's beginning to feel like exactly that: *waiting*. I want to go do the things that pull at me: my counseling, my photography, my writing. I've decided to take early retirement sometime this year."

For a minute she doesn't speak. Then a little smile breaks

through. "I'm going to have to get used to this. After 16 years you feel like one of the foundations of the agency. But I hear what you're saying. I hope when I'm your age I'll have the courage to follow my heart the way you're doing now."

CLOSURE

On my way to Schiphol Airport, I pass at least six white storks, each perched on its own light fixture, elegant and aloof above the busy highway. I laugh out loud and greet them, "Hello, beautiful ones!"

I love the storks, the sight of them always lightens my heart and feels like a good omen.

My stepfather emerges from the customs hall at the airport, walking hesitantly, using a bright purple metallic cane. I grin, my sister Kate must have bought it for him. Purple is definitely not his style, but he wouldn't care.

Somehow, in my mind, even though I had witnessed him age through the years, he has always remained larger than life, a huge, threatening bear of a man. Now he looks frail and unsure of himself, his trousers flopping around his thin legs.

He hates growing old. He refuses to remember his birthday, colors his thinning hair, and passed a second driver's test at the age of 90. He does his calisthenics every morning the exact same way he has done since college.

And now he looks like a tired, thin, old man. I walk up to him and give him a hug, which he returns with warmth. Then he breaks off abruptly and starts striding off with his suitcase.

"Let's go."

I catch up with him, guide him gently up towards the parking garage and my car, and drive home with him.

We're having an unusually cold and snowy winter. I have shoveled and salted a path between the house and my little guesthouse,

CHAPTER 4 - THE CRONE

where he will sleep. He looks at the path and shakes his head.

"I'm afraid I might slip and fall," he mutters.

He never used to show fear, he really is getting old. "The path is not slippery, Daddy. And you can use your cane to go back and forth to the house."

A few hours later we have both settled down in my living room with a glass of white wine. A bright, warm fire crackles in the fireplace. The wine and the warmth are doing their work. He sheds his usual reticence and starts a long list of complaints about his children, referring to them as 'your brother' and 'your sister'.

"They sure as hell don't listen to anything I say," he grunts.

"Stop complaining." I say, shortly, "I've heard all this before. Why don't you tell me something about yourself."

"Hmph", he answers, "What do you want to know?"

"Well, I know very little about your life, really. How did you grow up? What were your parents like?" I lean forward.

He snorts again but a little smile steals across his face. "Well, I guess I kind of like the idea of you showing interest in my life." He stares into the fire and starts talking.

He takes his time, speaking in a soft, monotonous voice. He seems unaware of my presence. His stories are about disappointment and shame – growing up in Connecticut, his father's bankruptcy, working on a lobster boat during school holidays, having to work his way through Phillips Academy and Williams College, and the bitter clashes between his father's Irish Catholic family and his Scottish Presbyterian mother that left him an atheist.

"I was stationed on a destroyer in the North Atlantic. We were somewhere up near Greenland when the captain called me up to the bridge. A telegram had arrived saying that my mother had died of lung cancer. And those damn Catholics, my father's family, decided she should be buried in the family plot, in a Catholic graveyard. The funeral was in a Catholic church."

He takes a deep breath. "The captain offered to give me leave to go to the funeral. I refused the leave. I refused to go to my mother's funeral because it was in a Catholic church."
Then his stories turn to my mother, the beautiful divorced woman with a two-year-old daughter, who came into his life.

"And so I married your mother and she came down with you to the Naval base in Charleston. We had a little house, the kind they allotted to married officers. You were two years old. I used to give you breakfast so your mother could sleep in.

One morning you didn't want to eat your oatmeal. I was in a hurry and got angry with you. You started screaming and refusing to eat." He stops and takes another sip of his wine, his memories weighing heavily on his shoulders.

"And then I... I did something with the oatmeal."

"You threw the bowl of oatmeal in my face." I look at him carefully.

"Something like that," he mumbles and avoids my eyes.

I let the silence deepen between us.

"You were always running away," he says, hesitantly.

"I was terrified of you," I say softly.

"I guess you had good reason to be," he answers, still staring into the fire.

When I take him back to Schiphol Airport, two weeks later, we embrace. Then he breaks off abruptly and goes striding off to the gate, leaning on his purple cane, his trousers flopping around his thin legs.

I no longer need to be afraid of him or angry with him. I no longer feel the urge to impress him. We have made our peace with each other.

I enter the beautiful open hall with its smooth wooden floor. The

CHAPTER 4 - THE CRONE

5Rhythms dance teacher looks up from her deejay equipment and opens her arms to embrace me. We have become good friends since I started dancing five years ago. I had come to love this expressive form of movement meditation, which has helped me to ground into my own body.

I whisper to her quickly, before the other dancers arrive.

"My stepfather died a few days ago in the States. We had a troubled relationship and I feel numbed. Not sad, just a sense of something moving under the surface that I can't grasp. I need to dance this out and I'm not sure how I'll react. I figured I'd better warn you beforehand."

She smiles, bright blue eyes lighting up her round face.

"That's what the dance is for, isn't it? Don't worry, I'll make sure that space is held for you to do whatever is needed."

I move into a corner, slowly letting my body get used to movement, breath, music, and the room, slowly filling up with dancers.

The music starts slowly, the first rhythm is *Flowing*. I breathe into my bare feet and let them travel in slow circles on the smooth wood floor. Focusing inwards, I give myself permission to inhabit my body as fully as possible, to be present in this space, at this time, as wholly as possible. My body sways to the gentle rhythm and I let go of all thoughts and let the music take over. Occasionally my feet meet other pairs of feet and we move together, breathe together, and then separate again.

The music shifts into the *Staccato* rhythm. My hips start moving to the driving beat as I search inside me for fire: the fire of passion or maybe the fire of anger. The emotion that comes is frustration. Why were we never able to communicate properly? Why did I have to spend half my life running away from him and the other half healing the wounds inflicted by him? Couldn't it have been done any other way? Couldn't I have tried harder to close the gap between us? Why couldn't we love each other? Why? My feet pound the floor and my angry hands and hips keep all other dancers at a distance. Boundaries! As a child I learned to set boundaries the hard way, by biting the hand that fed me… and slapped me.

Then the music shifts again and grows more frantic. It's time to let go of all control and slip into the rhythm of *Chaos*. I surrender to the wave, crashing over my head, pulling me into the water. My head sways and my body shakes, I can no longer keep my eyes open and so I stay in one spot, shifting my feet rhythmically, left, right, left, right, breathe in, breathe out… I see my body tumbling in the angry water, rolling over and over. My arms reach out to the light.

And I open my eyes and see the entire room of dancers gathered in a circle around me, supporting my desperate dance with their energy. I smile and reach out to them as the rhythm of the music turns to *Lyrical*. I dance in turn with each and every one of them, accepting all that has happened to me and all that is happening inside me now.

Gradually the music slows into the rhythm of *Stillness*. I breathe deeply and slow down. Supported by a dancer on each side of me, I let my body just barely move, following the inner movement of my breath and beating heart. Then the evocative song, *On the Other Side of Here*, starts up.

'There's a place I know
Only I can go
And no one else can go there for me […] [3]

---

3. Copyright © Chloe Goodchild,

CHAPTER 4 - THE CRONE

The tears finally start falling, unchecked, pouring down my face, washing my heart clean. I cry for myself, I cry for my stepfather, I cry for us all. The two dancers with me hold me lightly but firmly, letting me know they are there for me. I whisper goodbye to Daddy, who taught me so much about my capacity to be strong and fierce, to stand my own ground.

YEARNING

I have just turned 64 and am living with my cat, in my peaceful home in the Brabant countryside. I think back on my two failed marriages and other relationships. One thought that comes to me, is that my first love had been the purest of them all. I wonder how he is and idly type his name into Facebook. I immediately recognize his profile photograph.

Sam remarried some years ago after several failed relationships. Their life together has been badly hit by natural disasters and, traumatized, they now live together as brother and sister. He is overjoyed to hear from me.

As weeks of emailing, phone calls, and Skype progress, we find ourselves falling in love all over again. It's exhilarating. It's scary. It might be the stupidest thing I've ever done.

"My soul knows your soul. Even if we never see each other again, I'm happy." I whisper to his face in the Skype screen.

He cups his hands and reaches out to my face on the screen. "I have always loved you. We are coming full circle now."

His wife is not oblivious to what's going on. "She's demanded I choose between you. I have to let her know by tomorrow. I'm dying like this. I want to live. I need to be with you. Will you give me the strength to do what needs to be done?" The words race over the chat screen.

"I will give you whatever you need and love you no matter

what you decide." I promise. "But we need to see each other in person before you take drastic steps."

Finally, we decide to bite the bullet. I will fly to the States to meet with him. We will see if the old magic is still alive. He asks if I still wear patchouli oil.

The message glares in my face. He needs to honor his vows to his wife. I mustn't go to see him, we mustn't speak to each other again. We must break off all communication immediately. He's terribly sorry.

Deep in my heart of hearts, you will live forever.

I drown my anger and sorrow in wine and erase every trace of him from my computer and from my life.

I'm standing on the seashore, watching waves roll in and crash on the beach. Each wave tugs at my bare feet, pulling the sand out from under it, tickling my soles. The sun is setting and the light slants over the water, turning it to molten gold. There, where the sun is going, lies the country I was born and raised, the country where Sam lives. The setting sun makes a path across the water. A path I am not able to walk.

"You came into my life one more time to teach me how vulnerable I am, how much I yearn for love. There is no way to avoid heartbreak. It will happen again and again," I whisper to the West. "Goodbye and thank you for this lesson. Go with love."

DRAGONFLIES AND STORKS

I sit quietly, trying to study the dragon facing me, having trouble lifting my eyes. The dragon is small, as dragons go, not much bigger than I am. She has shiny green scales with a tinge of blue in them. On top of a long snaky neck is a jag-

CHAPTER 4 - THE CRONE

ged, pointy face and large, hissing mouth. She reminds me of a velociraptor. Her many-faceted eyes glitter with all the colors of the rainbow. The dragon is my demon, the demon of my self-destructive anger.

Slowly, I raise my eyes to meet hers, and immediately fight down my faintness. The dragon hisses again, rotten-smelling steam rolling out from her belly towards me.

I take a deep breath. "What do you want?" I demand, staring directly into the dragon's swirling eyes.

The green dragon snorts with laughter, "You, of course! I want you to surrender yourself totally to me and be my slave!"

My voice trembles. "What do you need of me, that I must be your slave?"

The dragon studies me. Fire comes rumbling up through her nostrils and she grins gleefully as I pull back. "I need to feed on your anger and your power, until you are weak and trembling. I need to fuel my flame with you, my flame is not hot enough otherwise."

I shrink from the hot flames that lick at the air around me. I steady my voice and meet the dragon's eyes again. "And if I allow you to feed on me, if I give you what you want, how will you feel then?"

The dragon rears back, towering above me. Then she drops and crouches down low, moving forward until her snout almost touches my feet. "I will burn brightly and fiercely." Her voice drops and comes out as a low rumble, "I will know what love is."

"Then you may feed on me, so that you may know what love is." I drop to the ground and stretch out, opening up and melting to the dragon's heat. The dragon begins to feed greedily on my slowly melting body. And as she feeds, something very strange happens. She begins to shrink, her body becoming long and narrow, her wings growing thin. So thin that they turn into gossamer wings. Only her head is reminiscent of a dragon.

The dragonfly hovers over the melted heap that was me, fanning it with her wings. And slowly my form coalesces and becomes more solid. I sit up slowly, shaking my head. I see the dragonfly, smile and stand up.

A two-year-old girl comes running to me. I pick her up and hold her close. She clasps her arms around my neck and I breathe in the smell of salt sea in her reddish-brown curls. As we walk away, the iridescent blue-and-green dragonfly hovers around us and occasionally rests on my shoulder.

In the waiting room, I study the people coming in and going out. The prim, grey-haired woman anxiously looking around to see how others react to her. The young woman with her wide rolls of fat under floppy clothing, ankles swollen over flip-flops, head bent over her smartphone. The good-natured, mustached man in his 80s, fidgeting at the long wait.

When I was a child, I didn't dare study people, they always felt overwhelming. As I grew up, I only saw people through the projections of my own anxiety. This one could hurt me. This one could ignore me. This one could cling to me and trap me. And now I can see people for who they are. The seeing sometimes elates me. Sometimes it saddens me.

It's my turn and I enter the room for my blood test. I've been

CHAPTER 4 - THE CRONE

feeling run down recently, a reminder that my body is growing old. The blood spurts gladly into the glass vial. She asks me if I take blood thinners. No, my blood is thin. My veins are thin. My skin is thin. I'm as transparent as glass. I always wanted this transparency and I have learned to leave off my protective armor. But it makes me feel so very vulnerable.

At the spiritual center, women start filtering into the elongated room with tall windows looking out into a courtyard. After introductions, each takes a seat on the ground against a wall. Grey Owl Woman smiles at the newcomers and gives me a little wink. She leaves her home in the Pacific Northwest regularly to teach Native American shamanic practices all around the world and, after attending some of her workshops in the Netherlands, we have become good friends. Her grey hair falls down past her shoulders and, under thick bangs, her brown eyes twinkle through silver-rimmed glasses. As she starts drumming softly, I sink down into my sheepskin-covered seat and close my eyes.

I'm climbing the stairs to a friend's home, another shamanic practitioner. As I enter the living room I hear her calling to me from the kitchen, "Madeleine, come quickly, I have something to show you!"

I step into the kitchen and see her out on her balcony, her arms around a pure white stork, an albino. "Take a good look at it, I'm going to let it go in a second."

She opens her arms and we watch as the stork spreads its huge wings and slowly soars away.

The drumbeat starts picking up speed, calling us back from our trance journey. I open my eyes, still marveling at the stork. Hesitantly, I share my vision. Grey Owl looks into my eyes searchingly.

"Tell me all you know about storks," she suggests.

I start talking about my love of the elegant black and white birds, how they migrate long distances, feeling at home in many locations. How they are both solitary birds, hunting alone, and social birds, flying in flocks and preening each other. I speak of the old belief that storks bring the souls of people to earth, the belief that gave birth to the saying storks are the bringers of babies.

She smiles, "And the color white?"

"I think that has to do with white being the color of the North on the Medicine Wheel," I answer slowly and thoughtfully.

She stands up. "Then it looks as though you have been given a name: White Stork Grandmother. Are you willing to accept that name?"

I close my eyes, feeling into a sense of wonder spreading through me. "Yes, I am."

Grey Owl Woman invites me to stand next to her in the middle of the large circle of women. She and the entire room chant "Welcome, White Stork Grandmother!" three times. I turn around slowly, meeting each woman's eyes, breathing in the acceptance of my new name.

LITTLE LAMB

I am holding a beautiful little baby girl in my arms. She has a delicate, puckered-up mouth and gazes at me with large brown eyes. My heart is filled with love.

I awake from the dream and think back on it, wonderingly. Then I head downstairs and sleepily start making coffee. The phone rings.

CHAPTER 4 - THE CRONE

"Mom? We thought we might come down for the day. The weather is nice and we can all take a walk and enjoy the newborn lambs."

"Of course, darling! You're more than welcome!" I hang up the phone and start putting the house into some semblance of order.

An hour or so later, Jamie and his wife are sitting on my brown leather couch, sipping coffee.

"We have to tell you something." My son looks at his wife.

"It's a bit early to tell most people, it's gone wrong before," she starts hesitantly.

I smile, "I already know. I saw her when I woke up this morning. It's going to be okay this time and it's going to be a girl."

Jamie shifts awkwardly on the couch. "Actually, we both think it will be a boy."

"We'll see. Let's go for a walk," I suggest.

We stroll along the dike, lined with pastures, filled with sheep and newborn lambs. An adorable little brown and white spotted lamb stands, trembling on spindly legs, bleating his fear and confusion. His mother, a burly sheep with a thick brown coat, is baa-baaing her encouragement from a corner of the pasture. The lamb suddenly recognizes where the voice is coming from and starts running towards her. Then his joy overtakes him and he bounces along, all four feet in the air at once. Bounce, bounce, bounce, like a little rubber ball with four joyous hooves. He reaches her and ducks underneath her belly to nurse, tail blissfully wagging away.

Six months later, I stand with my new granddaughter in my arms. She has a delicate, puckered-up mouth and her brown eyes gaze at me solemnly.

"I know you," I whisper to her. "Welcome little lamb!"

Roots

During my morning meditations the Mermaid/Witch voice whispers gently into my ears. "All life, human or non-human, animate or inanimate, is energy. All life is therefore connected. Let go your mind and listen to the core of your being."

I slip the blue and grey backpack off my shoulders, crouch down low, and drag the pack and my walking stick behind me. Even so, the thorny branches of the mesquite thicket tear at my clothing and hair. Once I get through safely, I stand up and survey the small clearing in the Aravaipa Canyon Wilderness. For the next three days and nights, I will not see or speak to any humans, I will not eat food, I will live without my phone, the Internet, and even without books. My only companions will be the non-human inhabitants of this wild land and my inner world.

It feels just right. The sun warms the dry, powdery earth and I can see a flat space that will be big enough to set up my shelter. A steep embankment leads down to a wide, stony area framed with tall, green cottonwoods. I can hear the rushing water of the river just beyond the trees.

A solitary mesquite tree, with wide, gnarled branches, stands guard above the three gallons of water I carried in the day before. I'm feeling a bit faint, a full day of fasting before I set out this morning is starting to take its toll. Slowly, I walk over to the tree and place my hand on its dark brown, almost black, trunk.

"I have arrived," I say, feeling the rough texture of the bark beneath my hand. I close my eyes and feel a sensation of warmth and peace flood my body. Behind my closed eyelids I see sunlight shining through green leaves, branches like widespread, welcoming arms, and roots. Tenacious, spreading roots, finding their way through rocky crevices, digging down deep into the earth, pulling up all the moisture this harsh land has to offer.

I open my eyes again, fill my flask with water, and then pour out a small libation at the foot of the tree.

Carrying my gear has tired me out. I set up my folding seat, ease myself down onto it, and relax. I sip water and listen to the sounds of the river, the rustling cottonwoods, and birds chirping everywhere. The sun warms my bones. I breathe deeply, letting sunlight fill my entire body and melt away the exhaustion. I feel welcome. Everything in this clearing: the trees, the dusty earth, the noisy, curious birds, the river – everything is welcoming me. I look over to the Mother Tree, as I have started to call her.

"Will you teach me how to put down roots?" I ask aloud. (There's no one around to wonder why I'm talking to a tree.)

She sends me a quiet affirmation. Not only have the last five days at the nearby ranch prepared me for this solo sojourn in the wilderness, my entire life seems to have prepared me for this.

FEAR

The water has stilled my hunger and I set up my shelter, using a tent pole, a tarpaulin, and several stakes. I organize my gear, rolling my sleeping bag up so that scorpions will not crawl in during the evening, sorting my clothing into two separate plastic bags and closing these securely. Dusty earth starts getting into everything and I resign myself to three days of dust. Then I sit back in my folding seat and look up at the trees around me.

The hammering of a woodpecker attracts my attention. I finally spot his striking black, white, and red colors in a nearby tree. A loud whirring announces the arrival of a bright red male cardinal. He hops about on a low branch, eyeing me curiously before he flies away, only to be replaced by his russet mate. I smile and offer gratitude to the universe for bringing me to this place of beauty.

Slightly behind my left shoulder is a huge pile of brush, fallen logs, and accumulated leaves. Something about its dark, tangled mass of chaos has already prompted me to call it The Witch's Hut. This is one of the reasons I have chosen this clearing. The clearing isn't just hidden and alluring, it's also a little frightening.

As I dreamily watch the birds, I suddenly hear a faint but deliberate rustling behind me, in The Witch's Hut. Suddenly I'm wide awake, my ears almost swiveling to catch the exact location and identity of the movement. Too much noise to be a lizard, too deliberate to be a bird. There it is again. My breath has gone shallow and a twinge of fear grabs my stomach. What is it? I remember the skunk the other day and suddenly have visions of a skunk strolling in and spraying noxious gasses all over me.

My rational mind grabs control of the situation. Why on earth am I afraid of skunks when there are rattlesnakes, scorpions, and Gila monsters in the Sonoran desert surrounding me? They are much more dangerous than skunks! But, deep in my heart, I know I don't have to be afraid of those creatures either. I have been trained during the past few days of preparation to deal with them. I force myself to breathe again and watch the sun set behind the stern, high rocks of the mountain across the canyon.

I can faintly see the headlights of a car, driving along a distant dirt road. Another wave of fear grips me. Suppose some crazed country yokel decides to cross the river and finds me? Images of the assault in the movie *Deliverance* emerge. It's my first night out and my imagination has hijacked my emotions. I'm terrified.

Slowly, carefully, I separate my consciousness from my panicked self and force myself to breathe. I ask myself what, exactly, I'm afraid of. The answer is simple: I'm afraid of the things that I imagine will happen. None of these are very likely to happen. In reality, there is very little to be afraid of. I am in a beautiful spot, in the middle of wild nature, and I am more afraid of humans than of anything around me!

I decide that, if my fears are a figment of my imagination, they can be allayed by the right kind of focus. I take my walking stick from its place leaning against the Mother Tree. When I go to bed, I lay the staff across the opening of the shelter and whisper a prayer to the full moon. I feel perfectly safe and that feeling of safety remains with me for the rest of my three-day solo. I never do find out what had been rustling in the thicket.

THE BELOVED

I walk down to the river, navigating the steep climb carefully. I sit on a large boulder, listening to the river's song, singing back to it and moving my upper body like water. When I close my eyes, I see water rising up among tree roots. Not a frightening image, it feels fitting.

As I walk back to my clearing, my attention is caught by a semicircle of large rocks. I count them. It will be perfect for my ceremony. I ask the rocks to please represent the men in my life. Then I go fetch the dried rose petals and other attributes I have brought with me.

I sit in front of the rocks and address them one at a time, starting with my stepfather.

"I suppose I hated you for years," I begin hesitantly. "But you were doing it the only way you knew how. And you taught me how to be strong. Even if that strength came from resisting you. Each person in my life is a mirror for me. You were principled and single-minded, and I see those qualities reflected in myself. And I also see your impatience and your ambition in myself. "

I take leave of him, gently and respectfully, and sprinkle rose petals on the stone as thanks. Then I move on to my natural father, Njørd, Sam, my first love, Anco, the father of my children, Piet, the man who had made me feel loved and safe, and even

Franz. One by one I thank them and let them go. Tears fall and I feel them rolling down my cheeks.

At the end of the ceremony I sit quietly for a long time, feeling the strong emotions cleanse my heart and soul of all entanglements from the past. That night, I crawl into my sleeping bag and fall into a long, deep sleep, under the bright light of the full moon.

The next morning I walk out, on bare feet, onto a flat stony area near the river. I ask for guidance: to let go of my expectations of ever finding my other half in another human being, to feel my passion and sensuality for the whole world, and to be able to experience the death of my old self. I lie down and cover myself entirely with a cloth, like a shroud, feeling what it is like to abandon all hope. A strange, high-pitched crying emerges spontaneously from my throat and I let it turn into a sobbing song. Then the song dies and I lie there in a trance state. Animals rustle nearby and birds flutter. An image floats into my mind of a little, round, sod hut with a tiny chimney. Another image of a pale, austere face of a woman, who turns into an owl: an owl-woman. When the images vanish, I slowly get up and thank all the elements for their participation in my ritual.

I spend the rest of the day lost in a sense of wonder. Birds all over the place: a russet-brown bird with a bright red beak, a tiny silhouette of a bird with a huge voice, and many more. The years I spent camping and exploring nature come back to me now. Being a part of nature, feeling, seeing, smelling, hearing nature. I have always loved this.

I sing Yeat's *The Tale of Wandering Aengus* to the clearing. When I get to the words '*the silver apples of the moon, the golden apples of the sun*' my voice chokes up. I feel such intense yearning. So I speak the yearning out loud, calling upon The Inner Beloved to show himself to me.

CHAPTER 4 - THE CRONE

The night is magical. At one point the full moon lights up all the leaves on the cottonwood trees above my head so that they turn silver. I listen to stirrings of night creatures and the hoot of an owl. Finally I fall asleep.

I have arrived home. I turn on the lights in the house but one of the lights is broken and keeps flickering. I pick up my cellphone and see that there's a text message. It's from the technical support, saying something about a glitch in the messaging service. I open the message and it is full of poetry. It's a love letter to me that I can only read scraps of. The lines of text fade in and out of focus, constantly changing, absolutely beautiful. The Inner Beloved has sent me an answer.

COMING HOME

Something has shifted inside me. My restlessness has disappeared and my yearning is less painful. I'm ready to stop searching, ready to turn around and offer my gifts to the world.

The Delta Airlines flight has arrived early at Schiphol Airport and there is no room for us at the scheduled gate. We sit out on the tarmac for 20 minutes while my befuddled brain, fried from 14 hours of traveling from Phoenix, via Minneapolis, to Amsterdam, tries to cope with the small logistics of airplane life. My cellphone is in my daypack, up in the overhead bin, which I can't get to. Somehow it doesn't feel like coming home until I'm able to turn my phone back on and listen to my messages.

A few hours later, my luggage safely retrieved, messages listened to, car retrieved, and having survived the morning rush-hour traffic, I leave the highway and drive through the tiny Brabant village, with its neat rows of houses, well-kept front lawns, and 19th century brick church.

I let my big blue Mazda drift down the steep driveway to the little white house at the bottom of the dike. As I get out of the car, I'm greeted by the exuberant trilling song of the blackbird and the chatter of dozens of little sparrows in the shrubbery next to the house.

Looking out over the fields, I see the traditional Dutch windmill in the distance. Everything is so lushly, verdantly green it makes my eyes hurt. My breath catches slightly in my throat. Surely I'm not missing the harsh dusty colors of the Arizona desert? The abundance of all this green vegetation feels somewhat decadent now. *An embarrassment of riches* – Simon Schama's phrase comes to mind.

As my key turns in the lock, a loud wail starts up in the house. I smile, my tiny, lithe, grey Burmese cat is already announcing her intense need for my attention. I enter through the mudroom and kitchen, pulling my suitcase behind me. SuuKyi runs up to me, winding around my legs and vociferously clamoring for cuddles. I scoop her up in one hand and she briefly hangs limp, a little grey rag doll, and then settles against my chest, purring loudly, and delicately kneading her paws against my neck. The neighbor has left the bowls filled with cat food and water and the mail piled neatly on the kitchen counter. The mail can wait… I take a quick glance around the floor; fortunately no dead mice, moles, or birds waiting for me this time.

Usually, I love coming home to my little house with its warm green walls, wood flooring, and huge windows. But I've been camping in the desert and the long flight plus the house make me feel closed in. So I quickly walk through the living room, throw open the French doors, and walk out into the garden, still carrying a contented cat.

The rich, honeyed scents of blooming white spirea and pale pink viburnum are almost overwhelming. The garden is full of color:

CHAPTER 4 - THE CRONE

yellow daffodils and forsythia, hot-pink blackcurrant flowers, white cherry and pear blooms. And bright, lush green everywhere – the rich green of the grass, the sunny green of the huge weeping willow with its yellow hanging catkins – so many shades of green!

I glance at the birdfeeders, they will all need refilling. Little brown sparrows and great tits, with their striking black stripes on yellow bellies, glance at me hopefully from the bushes.

I put SuuKyi down and she scrambles up the nearest tree. A large speckled brown feather is lying in the grass. I pick it up and recognize it as a tawny owl feather. I offer silent thanks to the owl. Then I walk over to my favorite tree, a huge spreading walnut, its bare branches just starting to sprout leaves.

I put my hand on the grey bark and whisper to the tree, "I'm home, I guess. Will I ever learn to grow roots into this damp, heavy clay, the way you have?"

I feel the solidity of the walnut tree under my hand, welcoming me home.

Verdandi pushes the sleeves of her blue robe back and leans forward to examine the web she is weaving. Her fingers trace the round pattern, spiraling in and spiraling out.

"She's beginning to understand," she calls to her sisters. "She has caught a glimpse of her wyrd and is trying to follow the path."

"She's finally accepted her pain and anger. The sensitive child within has emerged again. She is learning to balance the two sides of her nature: the mermaid and the witch." Urd starts spinning roses, dragonfly wings, and sea-foam into her thread.

Skuld carves the rune X *Gebo: gift, onto the bark of Ygdrassil.*

5

EPILOGUE

I walk towards the workshop tent with my bag of materials. Most of the festival's 80-odd participants are still finishing up their lunch in front of the kitchen tent. As I walk along, my eye falls on a large black crow feather in the grass in front of my feet. I pick it up, smiling, and drop it in my bag. It will be perfect. I feel awed and grateful for the sign, the birds must know what I'm planning.

In the large white canvas tent, I prepare the space carefully: setting out the Medicine Wheel with my felt wheel at the center and ribbons running out to divide the space in four quadrants. I smudge the air with white sage, and sing and drum to ask the support of Mother Earth and Spirit for the work I'm about to do.

People start trickling in for the workshop. Only six have signed up, many workshops are offered at the same time and the festival is small. I push my worry and disappointment aside, this will work with a small group too.

I stop drumming softly and smile at the participants, seated on the ground.

"Welcome to this Constellation for the Earth. I'm about to send you out again on a short assignment but I'd like to read something to you first."

I read a short text by Thich Nhat Hanh and an even shorter one by Joanna Macy to them and see their faces grow serious and rapt with attention.

I pause and add, "I would like to invite you to go outside for about five minutes and find (or let it find you) an object that represents part of Nature you hold dearly and is threatened.

One woman's jaw dropped. "I just found this on the way over!" She holds up a large pinecone.

"And I just found this on the ground in the tent!" Another woman holds up a large brown feather I hadn't seen while I was preparing the tent.

I laugh, delighted. Synchronicity has already struck. "I didn't see that feather, so it was obviously intended for you!"

The other participants wander off and return with sticks, feathers, or pinecones. We gather in a circle and I ask each participant to step forward, place their object on the center of the wheel, and say their name as well as what the object represents.

I start with my feather. "This feather stands for the birds who, along with the trees, were the only friends of a lonely child many years ago. They gave me the feeling I belong on this planet. If they disappear, my feeling of belonging will probably disappear as well."

A solemn quiet has descended on the group and I see how each person is moved by their own presentation and those of the others. I take them through the next step.

"Each of us experiences what is happening to the Earth in a different way. In the East… " I walk to that section of the wheel, "… we have the people who think, 'I wish I could do something. But I'm all alone in this and I don't see what I can do'. In the South are the people who think, 'Yes, the problem is dreadful. But I need to pay the rent, feed my family, make a career. I simply don't have the time and money. Why don't the people who caused the problem do something about it, they have money!'"

CHAPTER 5 - EPILOGUE

People start to laugh in recognition. I continue my path around the wheel.

"In the West, we have the people who are so angry and depressed about the situation they feel totally powerless. So they turn their backs, so as not to feel the pain. And in the North we have the people who are in denial, who say, 'There is so much evidence for and against this. I'm sure it isn't as bad as everyone says it is.' "

I ask the group to walk through the different quadrants, slowly and mindfully, feeling into each attitude. I start drumming softly and singing, accompanying them around the wheel, stopping sometimes to stand close to someone whose emotions threaten to overwhelm them. My thoughts have disappeared, I work in a semi-trance, a hollow bone for Spirit to work through.

After half an hour I stop and ask them to choose a partner and sit down across from each other. Each one talks for five minutes while the other is a silent witness.

Then the group gathers for the second constellation. This time I work with the different roles one can choose to take in this situation. The East is the place for creating new social and economic structures, the South for actions to protect life on Earth, the West for creating new consciousness, and the North for living individually in harmony with Nature and offering prayers and rituals to the Earth.

This is the first time I perform this, self-designed, ritual and I am amazed and awed at how strong the current of feelings running through the group is.

As I close, asking each person to take his or her object from the altar and find a place in nature or at their tent to make an individual altar, they share with me how intense and emotional this experience was for them. I give thanks for being allowed to conduct this workshop and send this intention out into the world.

Skuld pushes back her long white veil and smiles at her two sisters. She walks over to the ash tree and carves the rune ◇ Othila: home, into the ancient wood. Then she takes her iron cup from within the folds of her skirts, dips it into the icy-cold water of the well, and pours out a libation at the foot of the tree.

The mermaid floats on the ocean current. In front of her, she sees a large shape. As it comes closer, she recognizes a huge turtle, ancient and scarred. Their eyes meet: the mermaid's wide with wonder, the turtle's filled with calm. They touch, briefly, and go their separate ways. The mermaid turns to watch as the turtle sinks deeper into the indigo ocean.

I stand in a sunlit room. A voice whispers, softly and intangibly, "I love you..." over and over again. I know I'm not imagining the voice. I also know that this is not a person who whispers like the soft breeze blowing by the open window. I stand closer to the window to hear it more clearly. I'm filled with joy and soft yearning.

I wake up, remember the dream, and smile. The voice continues to whisper, "All life – human or non-human, animate or inanimate, visible or invisible, past, present, or future – all life is connected. All life is energy. Know this in the core of your being. Live by it and teach it to those who are ready to hear. Heal those who are lost and yearning to be alive. Celebrate life's beauty. And never forget: all endings are a new beginning."

CHAPTER 5 - EPILOGUE

The ocean waves crash endlessly on the shoreline. The tide comes in and goes out again, always constant but never the same. Ahead of me, my path stretches, some parts visible, some parts still hidden. There will be more challenges, more heartbreaks, and more joy to experience. I look forward to all of it. I get up out of bed and pull open the curtains, greeting a new day.

BIBLIOGRAPHY AND RESOURCES

BOOKS

Allione, Tsultrim, *Feeding your Demons: Ancient Wisdom for Resolving Inner Conflict*, New York, Little Brown and Company, 2008

Aron, Elaine, *The Highly Sensitive Person: How to Thrive when the World Overwhelms You*, New York, Broadway Books, 1997

Bellows, Henry Addams, *The Poetic Edda*, translation, New York, Dover Publications, 2004

Campbell, Joseph, *The Hero with a Thousand Faces*, Novato, New World Library, 2008

Campbell Joseph, *Myths to Live By*, Arkana, The Viking Press, 1972

Dilts, Robert and Gilligan, Stephan, *The Hero's Journey: a Voyage of Self-Discovery*, Carmarthen, Crown House Publishing, 2009

Mountfort, Paul Rhys, *Nordic Runes,* Rochester, Destiny Books, 2003

Plotkin, Bill, *Soulcraft: Crossing into the Mysteries of Nature and Psyche*, Novato, New World Library, 2003

Plotkin, Bill, *Nature and the Human Soul: Cultivating Wholeness and Community in a Fragmented World*, Novato, New World Library, 2008

Plotkin, Bill, *Wild Mind: A Field Guide to the Human Psyche*, Novato, New World Library, 2013

Roth, Gabrielle, *Sweat your Prayers: Movement as Spiritual Practice*, Dublin, Newleaf 1999

Sturluson, Snorri, *The Prose Edda*, translated by Jesse L. Byock, London, Penguin Books, 2005

Van Kampenhout, Daan, *Beelden van de Ziel: over de werking van de ziel in sjamanistische rituelen en familieopstellingen*, Haarlem, Altamira, 2001 (also available in English as *Images of the Soul: The Workings of the Soul in Shamanic Rituals and Family Constellations*)

Van Kampenhout, Daan, Tranen van de Voorouders: *Opstellingen en rituelen bij collectieve trauma's*, Haarlem, Altamira-Becht, 2007 (also available in English as *Tears of the Ancestors: Victims and Perpetrators in the Tribal Soul*)

Whyte, David, *River Flow: New & Selected Poems*, Langley, Many Rivers Press, 2012

Whyte, David, *Consolations: The Solace, Nourishment and Underlying Meaning of Everyday Words*, Langley, Many Rivers Press, 2014

Wormhoudt, Linda, *Goden en Sjamanen in Noordwest Europa*, Geesteren, A3 Boeken, 2008

Wormhoudt, Linda, *Seidr het Noordse Pad: werken met magische en sjamanistische sporen in Noordwest-Europa*, Geesteren, A3 Boeken, 2010

Youngblood, Robin Tekwelus and D'Entremont, Sandra, *Path of the White Wolf: An Introduction to the Shaman's Way*, Ardenvoir, Phoenix Publications, 2007

WEBSITES

5Rhythms dance: www.5rhythms.com

Animas Valley Institute: www.animas.org

Daan van Kampenhout: www.daanvankampenhout.com

David Whyte: www.davidwhyte.com

Linda Wormhoudt: www.soulritual.nl

Norse Mythology for Smart People: www.norse-mythology.org

Robin Youngblood: www.dreamingshaman.com

ABOUT THE AUTHOR

Madeleine Lenagh was born in the United States and grew up in Westport, Connecticut. She moved to the Netherlands in 1970. This book is her life story.

Madeleine is a trained counselor and body-worker. Additional training in Systemic Ritual®, mindfulness, and Voice Dialogue followed. After a long career in urban planning and project management, she took early retirement and opened a practice for life coaching and counseling. She works with individual clients and organizes workshops, helping people make difficult choices, process grief and loss, learn to take care of themselves, and live their lives in accordance with their soul's longing.

She shares her passion for nature with others through her writing, art and photography, and shamanic practices.

Passage of the Stork is her first book.

For information on counseling services and workshops:
passageofthestork@gmail.com

Website and blog: www.lenagh.nl

Photography: http://mlenagh.smugmug.com

Facebook page: http://www.facebook.com/lenaghcoaching

Twitter: @mlenagh

LinkedIn: http://nl.linkedin.com/in/mlenagh

www.ingramcontent.com/pod-product-compliance
Lightning Source LLC
LaVergne TN
LVHW041644060526
838200LV00040B/1700